INTRODUCTION TO ISLAM

Compiled by a group of scholars

Lantern Publications
info@lanternpublications.com
www.lanternpublications.com

Ordering Information:
Quantity sales. Special discounts are available for corporations, associations, and others who purchase in bulk. For details, contact the distributor at the address below.

ISBN- 978-1-922583-62-8

First Edition

NATIONAL LIBRARY OF AUSTRALIA

A catalogue record for this book is available from the National Library of Australia

In the Name of Allah, the Beneficent, the Merciful

TABLE OF CONTENTS

01 There is One Unique God

19 Allah is Just

33 Allah Sent Prophets to Guide us

65 The Noble Quran

79 Comparison of Muslim Beliefs to Christian Beliefs

95 Allah Sent Imams

131 The Hereafter

Introduction

The purpose of this short booklet is to provide the reader with a sufficient introduction to the fundamental beliefs of Islam, as per the teachings of the Holy Qur'an, and the Ahlulbayt (the Prophet Muhammad and his Purified Household). We hope that it will be a very useful resource for those who want to explore the Islamic belief system either as potential new Muslims, or those who want to re-discover their connection to Islam.

The Fundemental Beliefs in Islam

The five fundemental beliefs, pillars or roots of faith in Islam (Usul al-Din) are:

01.

There is one unique God: Tawhid

02.

Allah is Just: 'Adl

03.

Allah sent prophets to guide us: Nubuwwah

04.

Allah sent Imams to guide us and to continue the message of the Prophets: Imamah

05.

The Hereafter, or after we die, we will be brought back to life, to face the consequences of our actions

THERE IS ONE UNIQUE GOD

Section 1: Tawhid

1.1-The Existence of God

INTUITIVE KNOWLEDGE OF GOD

Deep in our existence, we have an awareness, an intuitive knowledge , of God. Unfortunately, due to things like being preoccupied with sins or vices, we can become oblivious of this awareness. However, in times of desperation, this innate awareness resurfaces.

Have you experienced a desire to talk to Allah (swt) more when faced with problems in life? This is because we are instinctively 'programmed' to turn toward Him, similar to a baby who finds rest only with its mother.

The Noble Qur'ān uses the example of people on a ship who are stranded in the middle of the ocean and faced by huge waves. They all instinctively turn toward Allah (swt) and beg Him to rescue them. When God saves them, a minority remain true to their promises to God, while others again become oblivious of God.

"And when a wave like mountains covers them they call upon Allah, being sincere to Him in obedience, but when He brings them safe to the land, (only) some of them follow the middle course." {31:32}

Though we are programmed to know Allah (swt), it is due to our lack of connection with much of our intuitive knowledge, our sins, and our love of the world that our awareness can become fuzzy and uncertain. We enter into a state of Ghaflah, or heedlessness, and become neglectful about what we already know to be true. This is where we can turn to the power of our mind in order to examine logical arguments that establish the existence of God for ourselves and others. In this lesson, we will examine some of these arguments. However, we should remember that learning about the truth is not enough to reach it. We have to also act upon it by staying away from sins and doing our obligations in order to preserve and strengthen our connection with Allah (swt).

THE TELEOLOGICAL ARGUMENT (DESIGN AND ORDER)

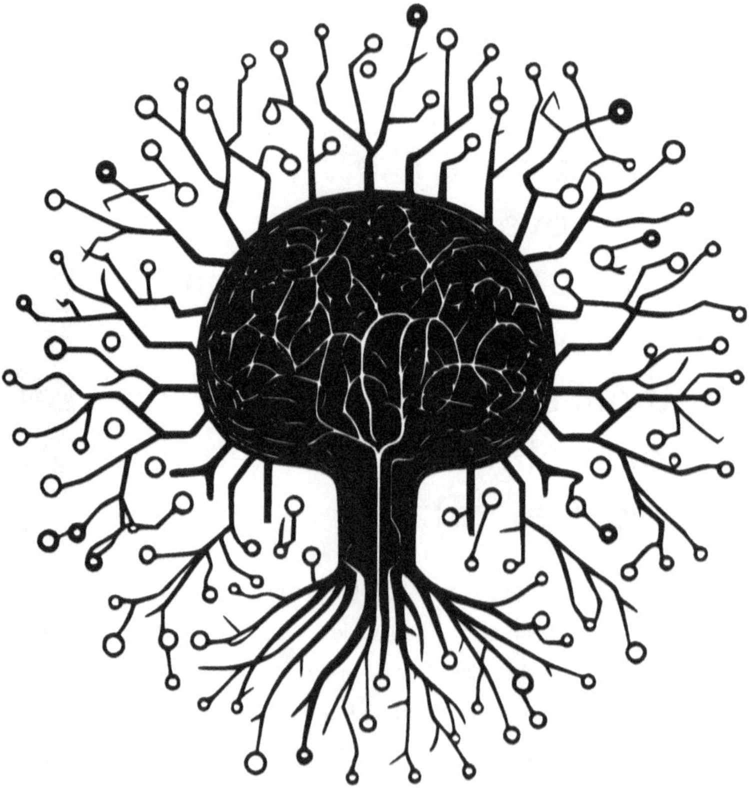

The world we live in is full of order. Consider the amazing network of neurons in our brain that controls all our bodily functions such as eating, sleeping, fighting harmful bacteria and viruses and so on. This system is so complex that it is impossible for scientists to create anything as complex as the human brain in any machine. The human brain is able to perform more functions simultaneously than any computer.

Another example of order and design is the way the planets are aligned around the sun, and the way the Earth is positioned in relation to the sun. Consider the gradual change of day and night. At dawn, light gradually pierces the curtains of darkness, and at night, light stealthily withers away providing darkness. Can you imagine waking up at a time when the sky is totally black and immediately looking up to see the sky as bright as midday? This gradual change can only occur because of the precise rotation of the earth along its axis, in the gentlest and calculated of manners, so that we feel the least possible discomfort.

There are numerous examples that go beyond the scope of this lesson. The possibility of such perfect order and intelligent law coming about by chance is so minuscule that any rational person would dismiss it. The chance of an ape accidentally typing a masterpiece when put in front of a typewriter is much greater than the chance that this universe, with all the order witnessed in it, came about randomly. A rational person accepts that such perfect order is only possible if the one who has put it in place is a Wise and Intelligent Being. This Wise and Intelligent Creator is God.

STRENGTHENING OUR FAITH THROUGH THIS PROOF

Imām as-Ṣādiq (ʿas) said: "The best of worship is continuously contemplating about Allah (swt) and His power." [1] The Imāms (ʿas) have also indicated that contemplating for an hour is better than worshipping for a year [2]. This is because it leads to one of the higher forms of worship which is continuous remembrance of Allah (swt). Allah (swt) states in the Noble Qurʾān:

وَلَذِكْرُ اللَّهِ أَكْبَرُ

"...and certainly the remembrance of Allah (swt) is the greatest..." {29:45}

Wondering about Allah's creation is one of the ways of remembering Him and discovering His attributes ourselves. When we see the amazing beauty and precision in nature, it speaks to us of God's wisdom, beauty, mercy, knowledge and power. This brings us closer to Him and increases our faith in Him.

THE COSMOLOGICAL ARGUMENT

Regarding Allah (swt) being the Creator of all, the Noble Qurʾān says:

"Were they created by nothing, or were they themselves the creators? Or did they create the heavens and the earth? No, they do not have certainty [in what they believe]." {52:35-36}

According to one interpretation, these āyāt ask us to ponder about the nature of our existence. Did we just come to be? Or do we have a cause?

The cosmological argument is a famous logical argument that has been presented in history that provides a response to these questions. You will inshāʾAllāh learn more about this argument in future years, but for this year, we will go through the basic argument by first presenting an observation and then drawing a conclusion.

[1] Shaykh Kulaynī, Al-Kāfī, Vol. 2, P. 55.

[2] Nūrī, Muḥaddith, Mustadrak al-Wasāʾil, Vol. 11, P. 183.

OBSERVING THE WORLD AROUND US

We know through simple observations that everything in this material world of ours depends on other things for its existence. For instance, as humans, we need food, water and air to survive, all of which depend on diversely interconnected ecosystems for their existence.

We also know that all the natural phenomena are interrelated and depend on each other. This is why even a 1-degree Celsius rise in the average temperature on Earth leads to such great changes across the globe: glaciers melt, sea levels rise, extreme weather events increase in frequency, rain patterns change, the oceans become warmer and more acidic, many species of plants and animals face extinction [1].

Because all the material, natural things around need other things to exist, this means that they don't have an independent existence. They may or may not exist, depending on the conditions.
In philosophy, this is called contingency, meaning neediness and dependency.
The first part of the Cosmological argument is to realize that everything in the created universe is contingent. This means that the universe itself, as a whole, is also contingent. This is because if all the parts of something share a characteristic, so does the whole. For example, if all the drops of water in the ocean are liquid, then the ocean itself will also be liquid and cannot be a solid or a gas. In this way, every part of the created universe being contingent means that the universe as a whole, is contingent.

[1] NASA. (2019, June 19). A degree of concern: Why global temperatures matter - climate change: Vital signs of the planet. NASA. Retrieved December 26, 2022, https://climate.nasa.gov/news/2878/a-degree-of-concern-why-global-temperatures-matter/?p

THE CREATED UNIVERSE NEEDS A CAUSE TO CREATE IT

The conclusion of the section above is that the world around us is contingent. It needs other things in order to exist. That means it couldn't have always existed (because it can't exist by itself) and there's no guarantee that it will keep on existing. How did it come into existence?

Logically, the physical universe needs a cause that brings it into existence. This cause cannot itself be contingent otherwise it too would need a cause to bring it into existence, and this would need another cause and so on to infinity! That means that contingent things cannot be the ultimate cause of the universe. Accidental phenomena (such as the theorized "big bang") also cannot be the cause for the universe because such accidental phenomena also consist of contingent parts, which are in need of a cause).

The universe also could not have created itself, because if the universe created itself, it means it would have had to exist before it came into existence and this is logically impossible.

This means the cause for the universe must be a Being who is not contingent. The opposite of a contingent, or needy being is a needless Being whose must always exist and can never not exist. This Being is greater than the universe itself and not contained by it. This being is God, the Creator of all.

The Universe

is dependent

A Necessary Being-God

Who does not need a cause or creator

THE CREATED UNIVERSE NEEDS A CAUSE TO CREATE IT

This is a question often posed by atheists. Once we understand the Cosmological Argument above, we can deal with this question fairly easily. We have just discussed that everything that has been created possesses the following properties and is contingent:

1. They are all limited. A table, for example, only occupies a certain area of a room.
2. They are all subject to change. The table will over time begin to deteriorate, break down and eventually cease to exist as we know it.
3. They are in need. The table is in need of the wood it was made from; the wood in turn comes from trees, which depend on sun and water.

We humans also have the same properties in terms of being limited. For instance, it is impossible for a person to be physically present in two places at the same time. We are also subject to change i.e. from birth to youth and then to old age and eventually death. Humans are also in need of sunshine for warmth, air to breathe, and rain for water.

On the other hand, God, the Being who caused the universe to exist, must be beyond these limitations and hence be needless of anything. He does not undergo any deterioration and is not limited by anything. This is God, the Necessary Being.

In part of his response to a question posed by a man about how God came to being, Imām ʿAlī (ʿa) said:

".....He exists without coming into being; He is before 'before' itself, before any limits. Limits do not apply to Him for He is the ultimate limit of all limits!" [1]

Since God is a Necessary Being, and is not limited and not needy toward anyone or anything, He is not in need of any cause. Therefore, the very question 'who created God' does not apply because God is not created. The Necessary Being, by definition, does not need a cause or creator.

[1] Rayshahrī, Muḥammad, Mizān al-Ḥikmah, P. 716, Ḥadith # 4126.

1.2-Attributes of God

ALLAH IS UNLIMITED

The previous lesson presented āyahs from the Qur'ān and provided logical arguments that God exists and that He is the Creator, or the cause, of the created universe. In this lesson we will learn about God's attributes in general, and about three of His specific attributes: His unlimitedness, His uniqueness, and His nurturing Lordship.

"Allah is the creator of all things, and He is the One and the All-Supreme." {13:16}

"He is the First and the Last..." {57:3}

"To Allah belongs whatever is in the heavens and whatever is on the earth, and Allah encompasses all things." {4:126}

In the previous lesson, we learned that every created entity in this universe is in need of other entities in order to survive. We also learned that the universe has intricate harmony and design. There must be a being who is beyond the physical universe but yet is responsible for creating and designing it.

The first āyah teaches us that Allah (swt) is the Creator of everything. He is the One who is al-Qahhār, or All-supreme, meaning that He is One for whom there can never be a second, and One who is not limited by any boundaries. The second āyah teaches us that for every beginning to anything that can be imagined, or any end to anything that can be imagined, Allah (swt) is before it and after it. The third āyah teaches us that every single thing is encompassed by Allah (swt).

From all these āyahs and more, and through logical reasoning, we can understand that Allah (swt) is unlimited. Unlike ourselves and everything around us, He cannot be limited by anything including space, time, and shape. When Imām ʿAlī ar-Riḍā (ʿa) was asked by an atheist to define the extent of Allah (swt), the Imām (a) said, "There is no limit to Allah." The man asked, "Why not?" The Imām (ʿa) replied, "Because if He is limited, it would be possible for there to be something added to Him. And if it is possible for something to be added to Him, then it is possible for something to be taken away from Him as well..." [1] Nothing can be taken away from Allah (swt), because that would mean that He would be like His creation, and dependent on someone else to give Him what He has. As the previous lesson demonstrated, Allah is independent and needless of others.

[1] Abū Manṣūr, Al-Iḥtijāj, Vol. 2, P. 396.

KNOWING ALLAH (SWT)

How do we come to know about the things around us? Usually we make use of our senses, such as our sight and hearing. However, our senses are limited even when it comes to material things in this universe. For example, even on the most perfect day with the most perfect flat land, the range of our vision is limited. Eagles can see 4-5 times further than human beings. Humans can detect sounds in a frequency range from about 20 Hz to 20 kHz, but we can't hear lower frequency sounds that, for example, elephants make, or higher frequency sounds that bats produce.

Are our senses capable of helping us to perceive Allah? If our senses are limited even in perceiving physical things, then they are even more limited when it comes to perceiving a Being who is not limited by space, time, and shape. Our senses of touch, sight, hearing, taste and smell can never perceive Him in His essence. They can however see Allah's infinite signs that He has put in His creation, and thereby be an incredible means of helping us to come to know Him. However, they can never perceive Allah directly. The Qur'ān states:

> "The sights do not apprehend Him, yet He apprehends the sights, and He is the All-attentive, the All-aware." {6:103}

A similar limitation exists within our intellect and our power to understand or imagine all concepts. There are many physical phenomena, especially those related to space and time, that our intellect struggles to grasp and that scientists still do not fully understand. If our intellect is limited in understanding these physical concepts, then it is even more limited in understanding or perceiving a Being beyond this physical universe.

ALLAH IS UNIQUE

From one of the āyahs quoted at the beginning of the lesson, we know that Allah is One in a way that there can never be a second. We can understand there can only be one being who is absolutely perfect through logic as well. Let us imagine, for a moment, that there were two gods who were perfect in every way. If so, how would we be able to distinguish between them? The only way we could tell them apart is if one or both of them were limited in some way so that they lacked something the other one had. This would make them imperfect and not perfect, and therefore not God. Therefore, there is only one being who is perfect in every way, who is God. He is Unique; He has no partner or equal and there is nothing like Him.

GOD HAS PERFECT NAMES AND ATTRIBUTES

We have established that we cannot perceive Allah (swt) with our senses or understand His Essence with our intellects. So how do we come to know Him? We do this through knowing the Attributes of Allah (swt).

We have two ways of knowing these:

- When we reflect on His creation using our senses and intellect, we see some of His attributes like His Mercy, Wisdom, and Power.
- He alerts us to some of these attributes in the Noble Qur'ān and the ḥadīth.

"Allah—there is no god except Him—to Him belong the Best [and most perfect] Names." {20:8}

In this āyah, Allah (swt) invites us to reflect upon His Names, which point us to His attributes. He also tells us that He possesses the best and most beautiful Names, because He is the most perfect being.

One of the great descriptions of Allah (swt) and His Names in the Noble Qur'ān can be found in Āyat al-Kursī. Here is one part of this description:

اللَّهُ لَا إِلَٰهَ إِلَّا هُوَ الْحَيُّ الْقَيُّومُ ۚ لَا تَأْخُذُهُ سِنَةٌ وَلَا نَوْمٌ ۚ لَهُ مَا فِي السَّمَاوَاتِ وَمَا فِي الْأَرْضِ

"Allah is He besides Whom there is no god, the Ever living, the One who sustains and protects all that exists. Neither slumber nor sleep overtake Him. To Him belongs whatever is in the heavens and whatever is on earth."
{2:255}

Whether it be Allah's mercy, power, life, protection, ownership, we should remember that each of Allah's (swt) attributes is perfect and unlimited in the way that Allah (swt) is perfect and unlimited. So, for example, when Allah (swt) says that He owns everything in the heavens and the earth, it means that He is the only real owner of everything. We sometimes think of ourselves as owners because we have possession of various things, such as a pen, bike, car, or a house. But the real reason why we "own" these things is because Allah (swt) has lent them temporarily. He can take them away from us at any time and when we die, we will part company from them!

Similarly, when Allah (swt) says that He is the Living (al-Hạyy), it means He is the only true Ever-Living being. All other creatures are alive at some point but not alive at other times, or their life is dependent, but Allah is Eternally Living.

Even though we think about the attributes of Allah (swt) to help us understand him in our own limited way, the reality of these attributes is above and beyond anything we can imagine.

pn

ALLAH IS THE NURTURER (AL-RABB)

One of the names of Allah is the Nurturer (ar-Rabb), which refers to his attribute of Lordship or Nurturing. A nurturer not only creates something, but looks after all its affairs. Allah (swt) did not just create the universe, but He also looks after it to the most minute of details. He graces us with life, moment to moment.

Remember, we are completely contingent and dependent upon Him, not only for coming into existence, but also for our continued existence. He is not like a builder that builds and leaves. Instead, an analogy to help us understand is that of a light bulb which always needs electricity to give light.

Some aspects of Allah (swt) being the Nurturer (al-Rabb) is that He is:

- All-Knowledgeable: He knows what I need at all times and in all situations.
- All-Powerful: He can give me what I need at all times and in all situations.
- All-Merciful: He loves me and will always give me what is best for me and what I need.

He is the all perfect Rabb, beyond our imagination!

Certain faiths believe that while God created the world, He left some of the affairs of the world to be run by other beings.

- The Meccans at the time of the Prophet (s) believed that the idols of wood and stone had power to affect the world and so they prayed to them.
- Hindus believe that god has three forms, and comes down to Earth in the form of avatars. They pay homage to idols as part of this belief.
- Most Christians believe that Jesus is the son of God, from the same substance of God, and that He has the power to affect the universe independently.

In Islam, all these beliefs are strongly rejected. Islam teaches that Allah (swt) created the world and looks after it Himself. Yes, sometimes He delegates some roles to creatures like angels, or causes things to happen through natural processes like cause and effect. Yet none of these delegates or processes has any independent power. They are all completely dependent on Allah (swt).

Allah (swt) created this world, and knows all its details. He is All-Knowing about this universe because it was He who created and fashioned it. He is also All-Powerful in the universe, and can do anything He wills within the universe, because it is His creation.

All other beings that people might take as 'gods' (such as idols or 'nature' or a certain human) are creatures within this world. This means that if they have any knowledge at all, this knowledge is very limited, and if they have any power at all, this power is very limited. How can a creature existing within the universe have any power over the universe as a whole?

The only being that can have real power over the universe is the Being who is beyond the universe, and who is the cause of the universe. The world we live in is full of connections and systems. It was created in such a way that each part depends on the other. For example, something as simple as the oxygen we need to breathe and survive, depends on a system that includes the sea, the heat from the sun, the mountains, the rivers, the trees, and even the soil on the ground. We know that God created this world with these connections and systems. Therefore, automatically it is He who is looking after its day to day needs, because He created these connections and these ongoing dependencies. It does not make sense for created beings to be completely in charge of certain parts of the world independently, because all the parts are connected.

ALLAH IS JUST

Section 2: ‘Adl

THE IMPORTANCE OF JUSTICE

Justice is to give everyone and everything their due right. Human beings are born with an innate understanding that justice is good and desirable. Allah (swt), who is All-Just, orders us to be just, especially in the way we deal with people around us.

THE THREE FACETS OF THE JUSTICE OF ALLAH

01.

Justice in creation

We believe that Allah (swt) has given a divine decree for everything to come into existence. With that decree, Allah (swt) also has given it a certain measure to specify its limits, shape, form, time, place etc. In His creation, Allah (swt) is just, which means that He provides His creation with whatever ability it needs in order to fulfill its purpose. Allah (swt) decrees mountains to act as supports for the earth, decrees humans the power of free will, etc. Each decree follows the limits Allah (swt) has set and helps creation achieve its purpose. Humans too are given different abilities and attributes, so that each can fulfill their unique purpose in this world.

02.

Justice in Legislation

We believe that Allah is just in His laws. Allah (swt) has created us and therefore knows us and our limits. For instance, He has created men and women with different physical and emotional capabilities and limits. It is therefore necessary in matters where physical and emotional capabilities make a difference (for example, when raising a family, or earning a living) for each to have different rules to ensure that both can achieve their purpose while remaining within their limits.

03.

Justice in Reward and Punishment

We believe that Allah (swt) has created the laws of cause and effect. Allah (swt) is All-Just when He punishes and rewards in this world and in the Hereafter. Rewards and punishments, both in this world and the Hereafter, are direct results of our actions.

The followers of Ahlul Bayt (ʿapl), unlike all other Muslims, have as one of their five pillars of faith the belief in the Justice of God. Our Imāms (ʿapl) emphasized this attribute of Allah in order to counter other's false beliefs regarding God's justice. Imām Jaʿfar aṣ-Ṣādiq (ʿa) said, "The foundation of religion is Tawḥīd and ʿAdl." [1] Some of the false beliefs regarding God's justice that the Imams wanted to counter include the belief that human beings have no free will but are rather predestined, or the belief that humans have no way of understanding what is right and good without divine revelation.

[1] Shaykh Ṣadūq, At-Tawḥīd, P. 96.

Justice in Reward and Punishment

FREE WILL VS. PREDESTINATION

Certain groups of Muslims believe that Allah determines all our actions, and therefore we are forced to do what we do. This led to such Muslims blaming Allah for all the problems that occurred in their lives and not taking responsibility for their evil deeds. It also led them to the following question: why would God send someone to Hell for doing evil when Allah forced him to do evil? In contrast, other groups believe that Allah hands over absolute control to us and so we have complete free will. Their beliefs seemed to limit Allah's power with this statement.

In contrast, our Imāms (ʿapl) have taught us that although some things in our lives are predetermined (like the natural color of our hair, who our parents are, where we were born, and our maximum life span), many other things in our life are under our control. We have been given the gift of free will. We make decisions based on our own free will. Although God knows what choices we will make, He does not force us to choose one option over another.

It is narrated from a few of our Imāms (ʿa) that they have described the reality of free will in this way:

فَإِنَّهُ أَمْرٌ بَيْنَ أَمْرَيْنِ لا جَبْرَ ولا تَفْوِيض

"It is a matter which is in between. It is neither absolute determination nor absolute free will." [1]

[1] Allāmah Majlisī, Biḥạr al-Anwār ,Vol. 5, P. 57.

Our Imāms (ʿa) have emphasized that we are responsible for our actions, because it was we who chose to do them through our own free will. Imām as-Ṣādiq (ʿa) explains this:

"Whatever that you could blame man for, is his action; and whatever you could not blame him for, is the act of God. God blames man for drinking alcohol, committing adultery, etc. Thus these are acts of man. However, God does not blame man as to why he is sick, why he is of a certain length, or why his skin color is dark or fair. These are the acts of God. [1]

This then means that when God rewards or punishes us in the Hereafter, He is doing so in accordance with the choices we made in this world. God has promised in the Qurʾān that He rewards those who do good with blessings and bliss. Those who disbelieve and persist in evil will eventually destroy their spiritual hearts and prevent themselves from being able to receive Allah's mercy, and therefore receive His punishment.

At the same time, we do not have complete free will. There are many things about our lives and ourselves that we cannot change. We have all been given certain abilities and limits to those abilities. Allah (swt) will only judge according to the abilities He gave us.

[1] Biḥār al-Anwār, Vol. 5, P. 59.

Now think about your actions in your own life. As individuals we each have power within limitation to exercise our free will. Brainstorm an action which you can take based on your own free will but is bound in some way by the limitation that Allah (swt) has placed on you. An easy way to begin thinking about this is to follow Imām ʿAlī's (ʿa) approach to the subject. In Nahj al-Balāghah, he says, "I came to know Allah, the Glorified, through the breaking of determinations, change of intentions and losing of courage. [1]" Think of your abilities and limitations outside of your control [2]. For example, you can choose what you eat but your stomach has limited space.

Once you have thought of a scenario which demonstrates the balance between free will and predestination, plan a skit to share it with the class. Two of your group members should act as characters in the skit while the third narrates and explains the balance between free will and predestination. Returning to our example, you could depict a mother and child eating dinner on a regular night and then have them exercise their free will to eat certain foods and experience the limitation of being full.

REWARD AND PUNISHMENT IN THE HEREAFTER

Allah (swt) confirms in many parts of the Noble Qurʾān that he will treat people according to their actions. If a person does good deeds, he will be rewarded with good, and in fact this good is multiplied and if a person does evil without repentance, he will be rewarded with evil. He never oppresses anyone nor treats anyone unfairly. He states in the Qurʾān...

"Allah burdens not a person beyond his scope..." {2:286}
"And they will not be oppressed so much as a single date-thread" {17:71}

These āyahs tell us not only that Allah (swt) will never be unfair to us in any situation, but rather that He will be Just when it comes to responding to our actions.

He also says,

[1] Nahj al-Balāghah, Saying #250

[2] Biḥār al-Anwār, Vol. 5, P. 197.

"So whosoever does good equal to the weight of an atom shall see it. And whosoever does evil equal to the weight of an atom shall see it." {99:6-7}

Allah (swt) is so Just that in the Hereafter we do not get the recompense for our action, but in fact get our action itself. We will see the reality or manifestation of the action we performed in this world. We will see our action as a creature or manifestation in that world, and we will immediately recognise it as our action in this world.

Let us look at some examples of the manifestations of our actions:

- If we make people around us happy, then when we are raised from our graves, we will have a beautiful friend to protect us. While other people will be terrified by all the horrifying things that are happening on that day, this friend will walk ahead of us and protect us from the frights of that day. [1a]
- When people are in Hell, they will be attacked by vicious dogs. The food for these dogs is the words of people when they backbite. When we speak negatively about someone behind their back, we are feeding the dogs of the Hell-fire that will then attack us. [1b]
- When we remember Allah (swt) and recite words of remembrance then we are building bricks for our castles and planting trees for ourselves in paradise. [2]

ALLAH DOES NOT DISCRIMINATE

Justice (or being fair) also means to not discriminate between people based on their characteristics such as race, nationality, lineage, age, or gender, no matter what the view of our society in general. Allah (swt) is the most Just and He never discriminates or favors one group over another due to their outer characteristics. He looks at all equally and the only reason for Him to look at one person more favorably than another whether in this world or the next is because of their commitment to serving Him.

[1] Leghaei, Mansour, Journey to the Unseen World.

[2] Biḥār al-Anwār, Vol. 8, P. 176.

This is very just because this means that all people have an equal opportunity to earn Allah's (swt) satisfaction. The Prophet (s) said, "Indeed Allah does not judge you by your appearance nor your wealth. Rather He looks at your hearts and your deeds." [1]

PRACTICING JUSTICE

Justice is the foundation of ethics in Islam. All other good ethical traits have some limitations, whereas justice is always good, without any conditions. If we want to perfect ourselves as Muslims, we must try to act in a way that is in line with the attributes of God, and as justice is one of God's main attributes, we should strive to be just.

We see many example where the Qur'ān commands us to be just, no matter what the situation:

إِنَّ اللَّهَ يَأْمُرُ بِالْعَدْلِ وَالْإِحْسَانِ

"Verily, Allah enjoins justice (Al 'Adl) and goodness (al-Iḥsān)..." {16:90}

يَا أَيُّهَا الَّذِينَ آمَنُوا كُونُوا قَوَّامِينَ لِلَّهِ شُهَدَاءَ بِالْقِسْطِ ۖ وَلَا يَجْرِمَنَّكُمْ شَنَآنُ قَوْمٍ عَلَىٰ أَلَّا تَعْدِلُوا ۚ اعْدِلُوا هُوَ أَقْرَبُ لِلتَّقْوَىٰ

"O you who believe! Stand up firmly for Allah and be just witnesses. Let not the enmity and hatred of others make you avoid justice. Be just: that is nearer to piety..." {5:8}

وَإِذَا قُلْتُمْ فَاعْدِلُوا وَلَوْ كَانَ ذَا قُرْبَىٰ ۖ وَبِعَهْدِ اللَّهِ أَوْفُوا ۚ

"And whenever you give your word, speak for justice, even if a near relative is concerned; and fulfil the Covenant of Allah." {6:152}

We can see from these āyāt that besides the general command to justice, we are also expected to be just:

- Even when dealing with our enemies or people we dislike
- Even when a conflict involves a family member or close friend

[1] Muḥaddith Nūrī, Mustadrak al-Wasā'il, Vol. 11, P. 264.

2.2-Tests and the Purpose of Humankind

ALLAH IS UNLIMITED

Perfection is fully realizing your potential, which for human beings, means getting closer to Allah (swt). If we look around us we'll see that everything including plants, animals, and insects, strive for their own perfection. They are all moving toward realizing their potential through continuous growth, even in adverse situations.

For example, plants continue to grow and struggle, and the strong ones remain standing even when the weather becomes harsh. An apple tree reaches its potential when it grows and bears fruit, but it does this instinctively as it grows toward its perfection. As humans, we have free will to choose whether to struggle and progress on our path to perfection to turn away from it.

Allah has given us 3 tools to reach Him and perfect ourselves:

1. ʿIbādah–Worship
2. Ibtilā'–Tests
3. Maʿrifah–Deep Understanding

TESTS: A PATH TO PERFECTION

As discussed in seventh grade, the only way for us to reach perfection is through seeking closeness–qurb–to Allah (swt). We must strive to reflect the traits of Allah (swt) and to become a reflection of Him. For example, Allah(swt) is the All-Merciful, and the All-Forgiving, and we should strive to reflect these traits.

Working toward developing these attributes in ourselves, will bring us closer to the true source of these attributes, Allah (swt). When we attain these good traits in their limited sense, we will get a taste of the absolute mercy, justice, forgiveness and Love of Allah (swt) and therefore be closer to Him (qurb). This is the purpose of life, and this is how we fulfill the true meaning of being the vicegerent or a delegate of Allah (swt) on earth (khalīfah). The best way to do this is to be on the path of Allah (swt), do what is wājib, stay away from what is ḥarām, and be in servitude to Allah–ʿubūdiyah.

IBTILA’–TESTS AND TRIALS

pn

Part of servitude to Allah (swt)–ʿubūdiyah- is to respond to the tests that we face in life in the way that Allah (swt) has commanded. In order to truly strengthen our faith and grow closer to Allah (swt), we must make the right decisions when we are tested. Tests are an important part of life and exist all around us in different forms. A math test establishes our math skills. A sports test establishes our ability in that specific sport. The most important type of tests are the tests that establish and build our faith.

This is because it is ultimately through strengthening our faith that one reaches perfection and closeness to Allah (swt). It is through tests that we can become the best possible version of ourselves. In the Qurʾān, Allah (swt) says:

الَّذِي خَلَقَ الْمَوْتَ وَالْحَيَاةَ لِيَبْلُوَكُمْ أَيُّكُمْ أَحْسَنُ عَمَلًا ۚ

"He who created death and life that He may test you [to see] which of you is best in conduct." {67:2}

It is narrated from Imām al-Bāqir (ʿa) that two angels descend upon Earth. Along the way, they meet one another in the sky and one asks the other, 'Why have you been sent down?'

He responds, "Allah (swt) has sent me to the people of this region to catch a fish and give it to the oppressor who has asked for a fish from this sea. So I have a duty to go after the fisherman who fishes at this part of the ocean and motivate him to go for fishing so that a fish from his work would reach that oppressor. This way he will reach his wish from Allah (swt). Why have you been sent down?"

The other angel responds, "Allah (swt) has sent me for a far more strange duty than yours. I have the duty to go to a servant of Allah who constantly fasts and stays awake at nights for prayer. His prayer and fastings are famous in the sky and I must drop his dish of food which he has prepared for his Iftar so that his test would become complete." [1]

In general, Allah (swt) has commanded us to be patient when we face tests. The Ahlul Bayt (ʿapl) have taught us that there are different types of tests and different types of patience [2]:

Imām ʿAlī (ʿa) said: "There are two types of patience. Patience with calamities is good, but patience with what God has forbidden is even better." [3]

01.

Test of Sharīʿah

This is the test of following the laws that Allah (swt) has decreed for us. If we exceed the limits God has set for us, we become unjust and not only do we suffer the natural effects of this, we also suffer the consequences of our actions in the next world. In this type of test (Ibtila') we are faced with the temptation to do something which has been forbidden by Allah (swt). Overcoming this temptation and avoiding this sin means we have overcome a greater test and have displayed a higher level of patience.

02.

Test of Afflictions

And certainly, We shall test you with something of fear, hunger, loss of wealth, lives and fruits, but give glad tidings to the patient ones. Who, when afflicted with calamity, say: "Truly! To Allah we belong and truly, to Him we shall return." {2:155-156}

[1] Shaykh Ṣadūq, Ilal al-Sharāʿi, Vol. 2, P465.

[2] Rizvi, Sayyid Sa'eed Akhter, Justice Of God.

[3] Āmidī, Ghurar al-Ḥikam, Vol. 1, P. 111.

This second category of trials- the difficulties or afflictions we face in life- has many examples including:

- The loss of a loved one
- Financial difficulties
- Illness
- Delay or failure in reaching a goal we had set in life.

A major part of our faith is how we respond to these difficulties that we face in life.

A major part of our faith is how we respond to these difficulties that we face in life.

We can also categorize these difficulties and afflictions as those that:

- Come about as a result of our own wrong actions or negligence. For example, a person who entrusts his wealth to a foolish person will lose it, but this is a natural consequence of his own action.
- Do not come about as a direct result of our own actions but are part of the natural order of the world. These include difficulties like natural disasters, as well as difficulties brought on by people or the society around us.

When we reflect on the types of tests mentioned in the āyāt and ḥadīth above, we can consider all parts of life as tests.

Every decision that we make says something about our character, and every moment of life is a test for us, because each moment may be a choice between obeying Allah (swt) or disobeying Him. Sometimes when life is easy, we tend to forget Allah (swt) and even this becomes a test for us. How we spend our wealth, like giving khums and charity, can also be a test for us.

Imagine two friends, Mujtaba and Ali. They both need to make a journey through rough terrain in order to get home. Mujtaba spends a lot of time reading about the techniques for surviving the rough terrain. He reads books and gathers very detailed knowledge on this subject before starting his journey home.Despite taking the time to learn everything he could, he forgets to put what he has learnt into practice along the way.

He gets flustered and impatient and rather than following the advice he learnt in books, he does what seems easiest at the time. Meanwhile, Ali learns what he thinks are the most necessary points to survive the journey and thinks about how to utilize them once he is faced with difficult situations. While he does not know as much as Mujtaba does, Ali remains calm during his journey and applies his knowledge when faced with challenges on his way home.

In this situation, Ali is more likely to achieve his purpose because he is learning what he needs to and putting it into practice; he is acting on what he knows. We can reach our spiritual goal of getting closer to Allah (swt) by responding to the tests and trials of life in the way that Allah (swt) commanded us to. A general rule that He has given us in these situations is that we should remain patient and persevere, no matter how difficult the situation is.

ENDURING TESTS

We have seen that many tests we face in our life are not due to our own doing. We may think that God is not being fair by inflicting us with these tests. But, the more we suffer, the higher our status in paradise and the more rewards we will receive. In addition, we have to remember that Allah (swt) gives more tests to those He loves because He wants them to maximize their potential which then results in them reaching the highest positions in paradise and being as close to Him as possible. Imām al-Bāqir (ʿa) said:

"One has a very high noble position near Allah. Allah will make him suffer a lot of calamities to reach that position. Lots of people will rush in to express their condolence to him and express their sympathy. If the people only knew what position God has granted him, they would have never sympathized with him, or expressed their condolence..." [1]

[1] Shaykh Ṭabarsī, Mishkāt al-Anwār fī Ghurar al-Akhbār, Vol. 1, P. 291.

When God tests us, if we remain patient, we will gain the rewards of being close to Him, as well as the other rewards of paradise. In the following narration, Imām as-Ṣādiq (ʿa) explains how a person who suffered poverty in this world is rewarded in the next world, as long as that person remains patient. Allah (swt) will say to His servant, who was poor in this world:

"I swear by My Honor that I did not make you poor to humiliate you. Now push the curtain aside and see what I have given you instead. When the curtain is pushed aside and he sees what God has rewarded him with instead of this world, he says: "O God! There was no harm for me due to what You took away from me (in the world) considering what you have given me instead (now in the Hereafter)." [1]

[1] Mishkāt al-Anwār fī Ghurar al-Akhbār, P. 712, Ḥadīth #1697.

ALLAH SENT US PROPHTS TO GUIDE US

Section 3: Nubūwwah

GETTING CLOSER TO GOD

A man wandering through a city, walks without any direction. The people around him think he looks lost, so they ask, "Excuse me, sir, do you know what you are looking for?" The man replies, "No, I am looking for something, but I am not sure what it is!"

We see that the man in the story is lost–he has no purpose. He has no direction. What if the man knew a little bit about what he was looking for, but not the name of the building or what it looked like? He would still be lost. If he knew the name, what the building looks like, and the directions of how to get there, we'd say that the man has purpose and direction.

Our ultimate purpose is to have qurb Ilāhi–closeness to Allah. We use the phrase "qurbatan ilallāh" to describe our intention for ṣalāh or for other wajibāt. This phrase means "for the purpose of getting closer to Allah". All of our worthy actions can be made into worship when we have this intention.

If our purpose is qurb, we should try to learn about Allah, because we are trying to reach closeness to Him. The more we know about Allah and about our dīn–the system towards Him; the Divine system–the closer we can get to Allah (swt).

We can use reflection about ourselves to attain this closeness to Allah (swt). If I recognize that all goodness in me is a reflection of those attributes of Allah and that He has the perfect, absolute versions of those attributes, it is only natural that I will try to change myself to be more like Him.

We all like to be kind, generous, and loved by others. Everyone is drawn to peace and justice, and when we recognize that Allah (swt) is the All-Just and that all justice is from Him, we will gravitate to this most perfect being, and get to know Allah (swt). He is the All-Perfect and He is the Truth, and everything that is perfect and true comes from Him.

Imagine that you meet a new person at the mosque. Initially, you might not want to expand your circle of friends and want to get to know them, but you observe that this person is very helpful and caring and kind to others. There is a natural goodness about them that makes you want to be their friend!

Allah is an endless ocean of perfection and greatness, and once we begin to recognize this, naturally, we want to get closer to Him.

We might even realize that Allah (swt) has placed within us the ability to develop some of His attributes in a limited sense. It is this divinely inspired, innate nature that we must develop to get closer and closer to Him.

LAW OF LUṬF

One of the attributes of Allah is that He is al-Latīf. Lutf is a subtle type of Mercy. Lutf is a specific branch of Allah's mercy (raḥmah) on us.

The **Law of Lutf** refers to Allah's lutf towards us. This lutf is a specific subtle type of mercy- in the form of religion- that guides us closer to His obedience and further from His disobedience, and stems from Allah's ḥikmah. Otherwise, if we discard or disregard the commands from Allah, we can be like the aimless person wandering. Our purpose is to seek closeness to Allah through His servitude and obedience, but we can only do that if we know how to obey Him in the first place.

As we discussed in seventh grade, it is with our ʿaql (intellect) that we realize there's so much we don't know, and that we need a guide. We don't fully understand what's good or bad for us, so we need a guide from a source that knows everything. This is why Allah, out of His lutf and precise grace has given us that instruction manual: religion!

If we pay attention to the world around us, we can see that Allah has provided us with ways to fulfill all our needs. For example, He has created thirst, and He has also created water. It wouldn't make sense for Allah to leave us alone when it comes to our spiritual needs. He has created the need, but also what we need to fulfill it–religion.

Religion helps us fulfill those needs and reach our purpose! Allah gives us religion because He wants us to become the best we can be and to reach our highest potential. This is from His lutf and love for us.

"Your Lord has ordained mercy on Himself." {6:54}

ISLAM: OUR WORLDVIEW

A worldview is a perspective or philosophy through which people understand life and the world. Everyone looks through life through the lens of their worldviews. We might put importance on viewing the world through our cultural understanding, or our age, or even our career path. These are naturally a part of who we are, but we should always have the worldview of Islam, because only Islam is from our Creator and can help us see the world for what it is and give us success in this world and the next, based on our responsibility.

Islam should be our worldview and be the lens through which we see everything. When this happens, everything will fall into place. For example, when we are choosing a career path, we will not sacrifice Islamic values to be successful, by earning ḥarām money, being unjust, or interacting with non-maḥrams excessively. If we have an Islamic worldview it will make it easier for us to make good and righteous decisions that help us get closer to Allah (swt) because we see the world from an Islamic point of view. For example, when we give to the needy we don't see it as a loss but we see that we just made a very profitable transaction with Allah (swt).

REMEMBERING OUR PURPOSE

As Muslims, we know we have an All-Perfect Creator–Allah (swt)–who gave us our dīn, Islam, to reach our full potential and become closer to Him.

Every creation of Allah has a purpose. As human beings, we are a special creation of Allah (swt) with the potential to reflect His attributes. This is a special potential for human beings because we have been given the free-will to choose whether to grow closer to Allah or to turn away from Him.

> "Surely We have shown him the way: he may be thankful or unthankful." {76:3}

We are trying to be our best version of ourselves by getting closer to Allah and following His religion. Following anyone other than Allah means we are worshiping something other than Him. We can worship many things without realizing it, even our own desires. True freedom is letting go of all these things and only worshiping Allah, who leads us to our purpose. When we have this higher perspective in mind, we can make the best decisions through this lens, even if the decision is difficult. We will realize that there is wisdom behind every part of our religion and that religion must be a part of every aspect of our lives. When people do not have this perspective, they think of religion as restricting our freedom as human beings.

THE SECULAR WORLDVIEW AND SCIENCE

Secularism is the principle of separation of religion from government. Some countries are very boastful about this practice, and it often leads to residents of those countries doing the same in their own lives.

If we take Islam as our dīn and worldview, then we will make every decision in our lives through the lens of religion. Historically, many civilizations around the world used religion as the foundation for society. Every decision was made using this lens. Whenever someone takes something other than religion as their worldview, they are actually replacing religion. We saw this in the worldview chart activity. Societies emphasize a secular worldview, which means to restrict religion to people's personal lives. This system is meant to keep people away from using religion as their worldview. Instead, people are encouraged to practice religion privately in their homes and not to bring their religion to public life, such as school or in the workplace. We may not see this at first, but it is often clear when we look at how religion is being replaced by other things, such as science or looking up to celebrities in some countries.

We cannot use our nose to determine the color of a book. This may seem obvious, but this is what we are doing when we try to use science to answer questions about God and His religion. We cannot use science to determine the best poem or how a person will react emotionally to a particular situation but people want to use it to argue against religion and God. Science can only examine what is measurable: empirical data. It is limited to the 5 senses. Yet, as we know, anything that can be measured or is made up of something else is limited. For example, we are made of bones and flesh, so if those did not exist, neither could we. Even at a microscopic level, if we are made of atoms, if atoms did not exist, then we wouldn't exist. If God was made of something else, then He would be dependent on that thing, which would limit Him. God cannot be limited in this way, but the secular perspective tells us that this material world is the most important.

Science is only meant to be a tool to measure the material world. Islamic civilizations have made many scientific advancements while having faith in Allah. From advancing the astrolabe–a tool that determines time from constellations- to creating the first modern camera, Muslims have been at the forefront of scientific advancements. Even today, they have made advancements in medicine and stem-cell research, always while maintaining the worldview of Islam. Science and Islam do not contradict each other, but science can never take the place of religion. Rather, science is one of the ways of getting closer to Allah (swt) by appreciating His signs in creation.

THE SECULAR WORLDVIEW AND CONSUMERISM

A part of the secular worldview is consumerism, which encourages people to buy more than what they need. This can be a worldview that replaces religion. When we want to have more, then our goal will be endless. We see this in advertising, when brands want to sell us products that we don't need. Companies want us to think that more material wealth will allow us to purchase more things, which will make us happy. Yet, true contentment can only come from our connection to Allah and reflecting His attributes.

Being "content" and being "happy" are not necessarily the same. When you are content, you are at peace with your surroundings, even if they make you sad. After the battle of Karbala, in the famous sermon of Sayyidah Zaynab in the courtyard of Yazīd, she said, "I saw nothing but beauty." We know that she mourned the loss of her beloved brother and Imām, and the fallen soldiers of his army, but she also knew that she was on the side of truth and was content with what had befallen her on this path..

We will never truly be content with the material world, because it is limited, and not the tool for reaching true contentment. As humans, we naturally look for the unlimited and the infinite because of our fitrah. When we make our purpose something that is limited, we will never be satisfied. In every action in our day, we should always use the worldview of Islam, and be vigilant when we are presented with other worldviews. We hope, then, to fulfill our purpose and become our best selves by reaching closeness to Allah.

CONCLUSION

To truly investigate and find a way of life, we must first examine how people make their decisions. Many people use their own philosophy and perception of life (their worldview) to guide all of their decisions. We should be aware and hold ourselves accountable in our daily actions and decisions, making sure that we are using the Islamic worldview to make our decisions. Our primary responsibility, which is dictated by the purpose of our lives, is to fulfill the obligations Allah (swt) has dictated for us.

3.2- Prophets and their Characteristics

PROOF (ḤUJJAH) OF GOD

The concept of religion is founded on the fact that God sent Prophets to humankind to guide them towards living the best possible life they can in this world, and to make it easier for them to reach their purpose. For every community throughout the ages, God has sent proof for (or against) that community in the form of a Prophet or the successor of a Prophet. This includes all communities throughout history without exception. This proof of God is called a ḥujjah in Arabic. Without the presence of a proof in a community, it would not be logical to have expectations that the community should follow the message of God.

A prophet or their successor is a proof for (or against) the people of their time because:

- The prophets and their successors deliver and teach the message of God in a clear and certain way.
- They put the message of God into practice in their daily lives.
- They perform miraculous acts with the permission of Allah (swt). These miracles prove that these prophets or Imams are not liars and are truly sent by God

If a community disbelieves in Allah and fails to follow His instructions, they can't use the excuse of the message not being clear, or not having a person they could follow. Allah refers to the concept of the prophets being a proof, or a ḥujjah, in this āyah:

> "[We revealed to] apostles, as bearers of good news and warners, so that mankind may not have any argument (ḥujjah) against Allah, after the [sending of the] apostles; and Allah is all-mighty, all-wise." {4:165}

Prophet Muḥammad (s) was the seal of the Prophets (the final prophet). Therefore, he is the Ḥujjah for all people who have lived since his time. This is because:

- His miracle- the Noble Qur'ān- is a miracle not just for his time but for all times and generations.
- We have ready access to knowing how he and his successors (the Imāms of the Ahl al-Bayt) lived their lives and practiced the message of Islam.

His successors, the Imāms (ʿa) were the living proofs of God for each time that they lived in, and the 12th Imām (ʿaj) is the living proof of Allah (swt) for our time.

WHY WE NEED PROPHETS

Living in this world, we strive for happiness and success as human beings. To attain the highest degrees of happiness and success, Allah (swt) has bestowed humankind with two tools: an inner prophet (intellect) and an outer Prophet (the Messengers of God).

Our intellect is capable of realizing some of the realities and truths in this world. However, the realities of the Hereafter, as well as some of the deeper realities of this world are beyond the scope of our intellect, especially when it is clouded by our desires and inclinations. Because of this, we need Prophets, who because of their purity have been given direct access to these realities by God. They teach us about these realities and show us signs for their truth, and help us to live our lives according to these truths.

Prophets are Guides

Whenever we are faced with a problem we cannot solve, or something we do not know, we turn to those who know or who have more experience than us and seek their advice. Think of how many times during the last week you asked your parents, teachers, or friends for help or advice, or googled how to do something? Similarly, whenever we are in need of guidance in matters related to our religion, we need guides, who because of their access to the wisdom and teachings given to them by Allah (swt) give us the perfect advice in all situations.

Our life is a journey towards Allah (swt) and the Prophets are the guides who show us where to go and the best way to reach our destination - like a GPS guide on a road trip!

Prophets teach us our Duty TOWARD Allah

The Prophets guide us on our journey by teaching us our duty before Allah (swt), our Lord and Creator. Imām as-Ṣādiq (ʿa) says:

"Surely, once one knows he has a Creator, then it is expected from him to also know that his Lord is pleased with certain things and displeased by certain other things. These things will not be understood except through revelation or through a Messenger. Thus, those who do not receive the revelation should seek the knowledge from the Messengers (of God) for they are the proof of God and their obedience is obligatory." [1]

The Best Life in this World and the Hereafter

As we discussed above, the Prophets have direct access to the realities of knowledge. They are not like the scientists, economists, political scientists, therapists, or psychologists of today who use their limited resources, knowledge, and sometimes guesswork to get as close to the truth as possible. Rather, Prophets have access to the truth, as it is, in matters related to both the Hereafter and this world. Therefore, their presence amongst their community gives that community the opportunity to know how to improve their life, both in this world and the Hereafter.

الَّذِينَ يَتَّبِعُونَ الرَّسُولَ النَّبِيَّ الْأُمِّيَّ ... فَالَّذِينَ آمَنُوا بِهِ وَعَزَّرُوهُ وَنَصَرُوهُ وَاتَّبَعُوا النُّورَ الَّذِي أُنْزِلَ مَعَهُ ۙ أُولَٰئِكَ هُمُ الْمُفْلِحُونَ

"Those who follow the Messenger...who believe in him and honour him and help him, and follow the light which has been sent down with him, these it is those that are successful." {7:157}

[1] Majlisi, Biḥār al-Anwār, Vol.23, P.18

Prophets are sinless (Ma'ṣūm):

We have already established two principles:

1. The Prophets are the practical examples that we must follow.
2. The Prophets are our guides who tell us what Allah (swt) wants from us.

These two principles necessitate that the Prophets must be sinless or ma'ṣūm. This will be our main point of discussion in this lesson.

Ma'ṣūm means to be protected from sinning and errors by Allah (swt). This does not mean that they do not have the ability to sin. They are still human and they still have free will and are able to sin. However, they have been given the ability to see the reality of sins and so they avoid them completely. If we could see that when a group of people gossip they are literally 'eating' the flesh of the person they are talking about, we would not even come close to such an act. One who is ma'ṣūm can see exactly this and therefore avoid all sins.

Why did Allah (swt) not give ordinary people this ability? Allah (swt), in His infinite knowledge knew that certain individuals would be strong in their will and commitment and would choose not to sin in this world. These were also the people chosen for the most difficult mission in this world–that of being a Prophet or a successor or an Imam. Therefore, Allah (swt) blessed them with 'ismah and inerrancy and this internal vision from the time they were born, because He knew that they would make full use of it, and because other human beings needed these individuals as their guides.

Sometimes, it may be difficult to imagine how a human can be sinless. Hisham b. Hakam was once asked what the sign of infallibility is. He described all sins as being under one of four categories: greed, jealousy, anger, and desire. He further explained that greed cannot be possible for the Imāms because he is the treasurer of all Muslims and therefore, has nothing to be greedy over. Humans become jealous of those who are above them but there can be no one above an Imām in status and therefore, they cannot be jealous. It is also not possible for an Imām to be angry at a worldly thing because their duty has been to establish ḥudūd and demonstrating worldly anger would be failing to enact the ḥudūd of Allah (swt). Lastly, Allah (swt) created them with love for the hereafter just as he created within us a desire for this world therefore, it is impossible for them to give in to worldly desires [1].

[1] Al-Amālī as-Ṣadūq, Vol. 1, P. 632; al-dodomi. (2018, February 21). Hisham b. al-Hakam on Infallibility. Shiitic Studies. https://shiiticstudies.com/2018/02/21/hisham-b-al-hakam-on-infallibility/

This is the meaning of divine protection or ʿismah. We can see from this that the sinlessness of the Imāms is not like that of the angels. The angels have no desire to sin, nor do they have the ability to do so. In contrast, the Prophets and Imāms (ʿa) have the ability to sin, but in each and every instance they choose not to do so.

WHY DO PROPHETS NEED TO BE MA'SUM?

Protecting the revelation:

If the Prophets (ʿa) could possibly commit sins or make mistakes, how would we know that they have not made a mistake or lied about the revelation? They are our only route of access to revelation and so if it is possible for them to lie or commit a mistake, then we have no guarantee that the revelation is in fact true. For example, if Prophet Muhammad (s) could possibly lie, how can we know that the entire Qur'ān is true and is the actual word of Allah (swt)? So if Prophets could commit mistakes or sin, the whole point of sending Prophets would be lost.

Being True Guides:

The Prophets are guides, and so if they commit sins or make mistakes, people would have no reason to follow them. Again, this would defy the very purpose of their mission and message. Therefore, the Prophets must be sinless and free from mistakes for the entirety of their life in order for the people to be able to trust them. Even before Prophet Muhammad (s) became a Prophet, he was known as 'The Truthful' and 'The Trustworthy', which later helped people to trust his word based on his perfect reputation.

The Prophet (s) used his previous good standing with his community as a proof against them. When he first announced his message, he went to the hill on the outskirts of Mecca and asked his people "Have you ever known me to lie to you before?" They answered "No!" He then proceeded to tell them, "Would you believe me if I told you there was an enemy coming from behind the hills to attack you?" They answered, "Yes." He then asked them to declare that there is no God but Allah and began delivering his message [1]. If he had not been of immaculate character previously, he would not have been able to use this as a proof against his people.

Being Practical Role Models:

TAs we established earlier, the Prophets are the practical role models of how the theoretical teachings should be applied. So, if they made mistakes or committed sins, we would have no point of reference, and would not know how to apply the teachings of our religion. In other words, we would no longer have a point of reference to tell us what is right and what is wrong. For example, Allah (swt) commands us to give charity. How would we know how much charity to give, when to give it, and who it is most important to give charity to? We learn all this from the lifestyle of the Prophets (ʿa).

We also see that even though we have an internal sense of what is right and wrong, there is still so much disagreement among humans as to what is moral and what is not. This is sometimes because people are influenced by desires or exploited by other people and their desires. Sometimes people do not know how to apply the moral truths they know. If it was not for the example of how the Prophets and Imāms (ʿa) lived their lives, we would have no point of reference for morality.

[1] The Message, Āyatullāh Subḥānī; Tafsīr Majmaʿ al-Bayān, Vol. 7, P. 323

THE PROPHET (S) WAS AN IMMACULATE ROLE MODEL

Now that we have established the above principles, let us look at some examples of how Prophet Muhammad (s) fulfilled the role of being a perfect example for others.

The Prophet (s) never stated something or made an order, without applying it to himself first. This was firstly because of his sincerity and secondly to give them a practical example of how to apply the teachings correctly. When the Muslims had arrived in Medina, one of the first orders the Prophet (s) gave was to construct the mosque. As the companions began to collect the stones to build the mosque, they were expecting the Prophet to stand back and take a supervisory role. However, he refused to just watch his followers build the mosque as a king might do. The Prophet (s) worked along with his companions, gathering and carrying stones from one place to another. A companion by the name of Usayd ibn Hudayr came to him and said, "O Prophet of Allah! Permit me to carry it (the stone)". The Prophet thanked him and said, "Go and bring another". In this manner he showed a glimpse of his sublime character. He said, "I am a practical man. I am a man of action and not of words only" [1].

Another example of the Prophet (s) practicing what he preached relates to generosity and charity. In the very early years of Islam, the Muslims were repeatedly ordered and encouraged by the Holy Qur'ān and the Prophet (s) to sacrifice their own comfort in order to give charity and help other Muslims who did not have enough for the basic necessities of life. The Prophet (s) practiced this teaching to its highest degree. He would eat only the simplest foods. He states himself that in the early years of Islam he would eat one day and go hungry the next [2]. He would give whatever he had to those who needed it or came asking at his door. This reached the extent where one day a young boy knocked at his door and the Prophet (s) had nothing in his house to give him- no food, no money, no clothing. So the boy asked for the very shirt the Prophet (s) was wearing.

[1] Al-Sīrat al-Nabawiyah, Vol. 1, P. 496
[2] Bihār al-Anwār, Vol. 16, ch. 9

The Prophet (s) closed the door, took off his shirt and passed it to the boy from behind the door. For the next day or more, the Prophet (s) was not able to leave his house because he did not even have a shirt [1]! After this occurrence, an āyah was revealed to the Prophet(s) about practicing moderation in giving. However, it still shows the level of compassion the Prophet (s) had for his community.

This is the way the Muslims took the example of the Prophet and this is the way all of the Prophets of God had guided humankind: through their actions. In his worship, in war, in peace, amongst family members, and in particular his manners with people, he was the practical example of Islam. Imām Ali (ʿa) describes the Prophet (s) as follows:

"Certainly in the Prophet (ṣ) of Allah (swt) was a sufficient example for you...You should follow your Prophet, the pure, the chaste, may Allah (swt) bless him and his descendants. In him is the example for the follower, and the consolation for the seeker of consolation. The most beloved person before Allah is he who follows His Prophet (ṣ) and who treads his footsteps."

[1] Kash al-Asrār wa ʿIddatul Abrār Vol.5, pg. 54

[2] Nahjul-Balagha, Sermon 158

3.3-Prophet Muhammad (saww)

IN MECCA

We have discussed some general concepts regarding Prophets. Here, we will specifically discuss the life of the Final Prophet and Messenger, Muhammad (peace be upon him).

The Prophet's mission began at a time when people were uncivilized and extremely resistant to any form of change. They would go to the extent of trying to kill anyone who proposed change. Prior to the biʿthat (appointment to Prophethood), the Messenger of Allah (s) used to frequently escape city life, and spend time alone in the cave of Ḥirā' which was located north of Mecca. There, he would worship Allah (swt) and ponder about His creations. Day by day, his humility and submission to Allah (swt) increased. One day, when the Prophet (s) was 40 years old, something very different happened!

Traditions regarding the First Revelation

The Prophet (s) received the first Divine revelation at the age of 40. This is one tradition that describes this incident of the first revelation:

"...When Muḥammad reached the age of forty, Allah looked at his heart and found it (to be) the brightest and the softest heart. Thus, He ordered the gates of Heaven to be opened for him, and sent the angels down to him. Muḥammad saw them, then he looked at Jibrāʾīl who was in an aura of brightness around him. Jibrāʾīl came to him, shook his hand, and said to him: 'Recite!' He said: 'What should I recite?'

The angel said:

اِقْرَأْ بِاسْمِ رَبِّكَ الَّذِي خَلَقَ.

"Read in the Name of your Lord who created..." {96:1}

Muḥammad (s) was overjoyed and excited. He came down from the mountain wondering if the pagans of Quraysh would deny his revelation. Thus, Allah (swt) willed to empower His Messenger with more certainty and hence he did not pass by any vegetation or rock but they greeted him as the 'Messenger of Allah'..." [1]

[1] ʿAllāmah Majlisī, Biḥār al-Anwār, Vol. 18, P. 184, Ḥadīth #205

With the onset of the revelation, the Prophet (s) started an all-out struggle to invite people toward the truth. This relentless struggle of his continued through the most difficult of conditions: from threats and numerous wars to political pressure and economic sanctions. Nothing diminished his resolve or frightened him at all. In a backward and hopeless society where racism, violence, and superstitions were prevalent—he planted the seeds for his nation (ummah) [1].

On one hand, he trained people one-by-one, passing on to them the pure teachings of Islam that he embodied; and on the other hand he recognized the reality of how Islam needed a political order to be able to attain its goals. Forming a government, forming an army, sending letters to other governments—all of these were indicative of his astute statesmanship. His ten years of ruling in Medina are forever recorded in history as a shining example of an Islamic government. When he passed away—23 blessed years after the first revelation—he left behind a community at the peak of power and dignity. This same system and community, within a short span of time, became the most powerful force in the world.

General Invitation to Islam and the First Muslims

Three years after receiving the first revelation, the Prophet (s) began inviting the general public to accept Islam. During the first three years, the Prophet (s) invited his own family and a few select companions to Islam. After this core was formed, he then publicly preached the message of "There is no god except Allah" and "Muhammad is His Messenger." He educated the people about the hereafter, life after death, and Allah's system of rewards and punishments based on people's actions in this world.

Many people found his words very attractive because they conformed to reason and logic. At the same time, there were others who reacted negatively towards the message of Islam and began to oppose it publicly and quite harshly.
Many people in positions of power reacted angrily toward the Prophet (s) because they realised that his teachings threatened their status and interests. They called him a magician who wished to create discord and disunity amongst them. They even urged their children to throw stones and garbage at him as he walked in their alleys.

[1] Nahj al-Balāghah, Sermon 2.

With a lot of forbearance, Prophet Muhammad (s) continued his message together with a few companions who had secretly accepted Islam before this general invitation. These included his wife Lady Khadījah (ʿaf), his cousin Imām ʿAlī (ʿa), and his companions: Bilāl ibn Rabāh, Abū Dharr al-Ghifārī, Salmān al-Fārsi, Miqdād, and ʿAmmār ibn Yāsir.

The leaders of the Quraysh, headed by Abū Sufyān, could no longer tolerate the Prophet's (s) message, so they decided to kill him and subject his companions to extreme torture with the hope of forcing them to surrender.

The Prophet (ṣ) did not Tolerate any Discrimination or Racism

One of the main parts of the Prophet's (s) message was that everyone–whether male or female, black or white, rich or poor, Arab or non-Arab–were only to be judged by their piety and God-consciousness in the eyes of Allah (swt) {49:13}. Muslims were asked to sit and eat together with the poor, accept their proposals of marriage to their daughters, and even share positions of leadership with them.

These messages and teachings were not taken very well by those people because it meant that they would have to change their old habits and attitudes at the onset of accepting Islam. Those who were being oppressed loved these teachings, but the oppressors detested them.

Once, a rich person dressed in clean and elegant clothes arrived in the presence of the Prophet (s) and sat down before him. A short while later, a poor person wearing old and tattered clothes arrived, saluted the assembly, and sat down wherever he found a vacant place.

The Prophet (s) had taught them that all Muslims are brothers, and in an assembly one should sit wherever one finds a place, regardless of any status. It so happened that this poor man was sitting right next to a very rich man which caused the rich man to gather the edges of his clothes around himself so that the poor man would not touch them.

Having observed this, the Prophet (s) remarked to this rich man: "Did you fear that the poor person next to you might make your clothes dirty?"
The rich man replied: "No." "Then why did you behave like this?" asked the Prophet (s).

The man responded: "I admit that was the most undesirable thing to do. It was an error on my part, and I confess my guilt. I have a companion who makes good deeds appear evil to me, and vice-versa. O Prophet of Allah! As compensation for this reprehensible act of mine, I want to give half of my wealth to this poor man."
Turning to the poor man, the Prophet (s) inquired: "Do you accept this offer (of remorse)?"

"No, O Prophet of Allah," replied the poor man.

The people who were present there were taken by surprise, they thought that the poor man was a fool, but then he explained himself: "O Prophet of Allah, I refuse to accept this offer because I fear that I might then become arrogant, and ill treat my Muslim brothers the way he did to me. [1]"

The Economic and Social Blockade

After several failed attempts to extinguish the light of Islam, the chiefs of Quraysh led by Abū Sufyān decided upon an economic and social blockade in the 7th year of the advent of Islam. They imposed terms and conditions that every person belonging to the Quraysh and all of their allies had to follow.

These conditions included a ban on:

- Every sort of trade with the Prophet and his supporters
- Association with the Prophet and his supporters
- Marriage with the Muslim community

The Prophet (s) and his companions were exiled and had to live in a valley known as the Valley of Abū Ṭālib that was near al-Masjid al-Ḥarām and behind the Ṣafā and Marwā mountains. They were forced to set up small houses and tents in this region. The blockade lasted for three years and placed immense pressure on the Muslims.

[1] Al-Kāfī, Vol. 2, P. 260.

At times, all they had to eat during the day was dates, and even that in such limited quantities that sometimes one date would have to be shared between two people. Even in such intense conditions, the Prophet (s) remained patient, calm and composed, placing his full trust in Allah (swt). Whenever he got an opportunity to preach, he did so. It was also in these three years that the wealth of Lady Khadījah served to keep the Muslims alive. She would purchase food at a high price on the black market and then distribute it among the Muslims. She exhausted all her wealth for the sake of Islam.

After three years of intense suffering, pressure built up against Abū Jahl and the other leaders who spearheaded the boycott. When the polytheists went to see the treaty they had agreed upon in the Kaʿbah, they noticed that it had been miraculously eaten by termites except for the phrase "Bismika Allāhumma" (In your name, O Allah). The Muslims were allowed to return to their homes and trade with the Quraysh was restored. However, just after their return home, the Noble Prophet (s) lost his dear uncle Abū Ṭālib and two months after that, his beloved wife Khadījah passed away. Even though the Prophet (s) had lost two loved ones, he showed patience and continued his responsibilities towards Allah (swt).

The Prophet's Patience

It was ifṭār time, and Anas ibn Mālik, one of the Prophet's servants, put a bowl of milk in the room and covered it with a piece of cloth, so that the Prophet (s) could open his fast. He had prepared milk for the Prophet to break his fast like previous days. Anas was starving and waiting for the Prophet to come so they could break their fast together. However, the Prophet did not return home for a long time. He thought to himself, "The Prophet must have been invited by someone [to eat with them]."

Seeing that the Prophet (s) was still not home, Anas drank all the milk. In the meantime, the Prophet (s) came back with some of his friends. Anas asked one of them "Has the Prophet broken his fast?" They replied, "No, he has not." Anas felt really ashamed and thought to himself, "What did I do? The Prophet fasted today and now he is starving. If he learns I ate his food, he may get sad or even angry."

When the Prophet (s) learned Anas had not left any food for him, he treated him as if nothing had happened. The Prophet (s) went to bed hungry that night, and he never brought up the issue with Anas after that [1]. Anas ibn Mālik was really ashamed and understood how the Prophet (s) had a great amount of patience. The primary goal of the Prophet (s) was to raise the level of moral conduct amongst the people. Hence, it was necessary that he himself be the epitome of such conduct.

In a lengthy narration quoted in the book Sunan an-Nabī, Imām ʿAlī (ʿa) narrates aspects of the conduct of the Messenger of Allah (s) to Imām al-Ḥusayn (ʿa). Below are some parts of this narration:

- The Prophet (s) would remain silent except when it was necessary for him to speak, and he would be friendly with the people and would not alienate them [2].
- He would be careful with the people and would be cautious not to be impolite or turn away from them, frowning. He would seek to know about the condition of his companions and he would ask the people about the condition of others (like their relatives or neighbors) [3].
- He was always cheerful, easygoing, approachable and soft-spoken. He was never rude or harsh. He never laughed loudly, never uttered obscenities, never looked for faults in people and never flattered anyone [4].

Miʿrāj: The Heavenly Ascension

The Prophet (s) achieved the most lofty spiritual station by personifying qualities such as ṣabr. This led to a unique achievement for the Prophet (s), the heavenly ascension or Miʿrāj.

Miʿrāj is a special distinction given to the Noble Prophet (s) by Allah (swt). It shows us his status compared to all other humans. This physical journey of the Prophet (s) began from Masjid ul-Ḥarām in Mecca to Masjid al-Aqsā in Quds, and then to an unspecified spiritual realm where he witnessed the heavens and hell and other realities.

The Qurʾān refers to Miʿrāj:

[1] Makārim al-Akhlāq, Vol. 1, P. 78; 250 Year Old Person, Āyatullah Ali Khamenei
[2] Ma'ānī al-Akhbār, P. 83, 'Uyun Akhbār al-Rid'a, Vol. 1, P. 246; Al-Sirah al-Nabawiyyah of Ibn Kathīr, Vol. 2, P. 601
[3] Irshād al-Qulūb, P. 115
[4] Ibid

"Immaculate is He who carried His servant on a journey by night from the Sacred Mosque to the Farthest Mosque whose environs We have blessed, that We might show him some of Our signs. Indeed, He is the All-hearing, the All-seeing." {17:1}

From Masjid al-Aqsā, he then proceeded to the skies (heavens) where he observed the stars and the systems of the world. He conversed with the souls of the previous Prophets (ʿa) and with the angels of the heavens. Prophet Muḥammad (s) also saw heaven and hell.

According to a ḥadīth [1], when the Prophet (s) returned, the Quraysh questioned him about this journey, not believing that this could all occur in one night.

Prophet Muḥammad (s) not only described the layout of Masjid al-Aqsā and details of certain things he had seen there, but also, to prove that he had gone to al-Quds, he told them of people he had met in his travel between Masjid al-Aqsā and Mecca. The Prophet (s) met a caravan who had lost their camel and he asked them to give him water and that he drank from their water. It was not long afterwards that the travelers of that caravan reached Mecca and reported the events that had occurred. [2].

A person asked Imām as-Sajjād (ʿa): "Is there a particular place [reserved] for Allah (swt)?"
The Imām (ʿa) replied, "No."

The man said, "Then why did He make his Noble Prophet Muḥammad (s) journey through the skies?"

Imām as-Sajjad (ʿa), replied, "He made him ascend so that he might become aware of the expanse of the universe and see and hear wonderful things, the likes of which had not been seen and heard by the eyes and ears [of anyone] before. [3]"

[1] Irshād al-Qulūb, Vol. 1, P. 199
[2] Forūq Abadiyat, Ayatullah Sobhānī, Vol.1, P. 379-381
[3] ʿIlal ash-Sharāʾiʿ, P. 131-132

3.4-Prophet Muhammad (saww)

IN MADINA

In the next sections, we will discuss some of the major events in the life of Prophet Muhammad (saw).

Islam Spreads to Madina

The two tribes of ʿAws and Khazraj had a long-standing enmity and would often have battles in Medina that would sometimes last for years on end. The people of Medina used to go to Mecca to seek help from the Quraysh regarding their tribal wars. On one of these trips, their leader heard the Noble Prophet recite āyahs 151 to 152 of Sūrah al-Anʿām. The recitation included the following:

"...you shall not kill a soul [whose life] Allah has made inviolable, except with due cause. This is what He has enjoined upon you so that you may exercise your reason." {6:151}

The words of the Noble Qurʾān affected him greatly. The man asked his friends from Medina to meet the Noble Prophet (s) and the news of the new religion spread very quickly among them.

Soon, during one of the years that the people of Medina went to Mecca for their pilgrimage, they formally became Muslims. Upon their return to Medina, they took great efforts to spread the message of Islam. [4]

[1] Irshād al-Qulūb, Vol. 1, P. 199

[2] Forūq Abadiyat, Ayatullah Sobhānī, Vol.1, P. 379-381

[3] ʿIlal ash-Sharāʾiʿ, P. 131-132

[4] Seal of the Prophet and his message.

Life after Migration

After migrating to Medina, the Muslims were faced with different challenges from the Quraysh and other non-Muslims, including hypocrites and spies among their ranks. In order to ease the life of the Muslims and bring peace between tribes and different faiths, Rasūlullāh established treaties with different groups. [1]

Another reason why the Prophet (s) established treaties amongst different groups was in order to spread Islam in a peaceful manner. There were a few obstacles in the way of propagating Islam, such as armed enemies and enmity. The Prophet knew that if the enemies were disarmed and no longer had the intention to fight the Muslims militarily, Muslims would be free to preach Islam, and the people of Arabia would soon become Muslims. Indeed, this is what happened. [2]

The Peace Treaty of Ḥudaybiyyah

In the year 6 AH, Prophet Muḥammad (s), along with about 1600 people left from Medina, heading to Mecca in order to perform Ḥajj. They did not carry any weapons with them as a gesture of their good will and to show that the purpose of their journey was solely to perform the pilgrimage. When the Quraysh learned the Muslims were on their way, they vowed not to allow them to enter Mecca and stopped them at a place called Ḥudaybiyyah. The Noble Prophet (s) sent an ambassador to the Quraysh with some gifts to explain the intention of the Muslims. However, in response, the Quraysh killed the ambassador's camel and put the ambassador's life in danger.

After many attempts to come to terms with Quraysh, the Prophet (s) was finally able to make a treaty with them. This was named the Treaty of Ḥudaybiyyah. Although most of the terms in the treaty seemed to be against the Muslims, the Prophet (s) accepted them [3]. The treaty included the following:

- There would be no fighting between the Muslims and the Quraysh for ten years.
- Other tribes should be free in giving allegiance to or forming pacts with either the Quraysh or the Muslims.

[1] For example, after arriving in Medina, the Prophet established the constitution of Medina to ensure that different tribes and people of different religions (like the Jews of Medina) could peacefully live together.

[2] Ja'far Subhani, The Message

[3] Sheikh Mansour Leghaei, The Revolution of Imam Husain

- Any dependent (like a minor child or a slave) who went to Prophet Muḥammad from the Quraysh without the permission of their parent/guardian should be returned to Quraysh but whoever went to the Quraysh from the Muslims would not be returned.
- The Prophet and his companions (the Muslims) would go back and not enter Mecca that year. However, they would come back to enter Mecca (unarmed) the following year for the pilgrimage and reside within for only three days. [1]

Some of the companions complained about the treaty. However, the Prophet (s) insisted it was the best thing for Islam. It was this treaty that paved the way for the conquest of Mecca which occurred two years later. Regarding the Treaty of Ḥudaybiyyah, Allah (swt) says in the Noble Qurʾān:

"Indeed We have inaugurated for you a clear victory." {48:1}

Quraysh Violate the Treaty

Two years after the Treaty of Ḥudaybiyyah took place, the tribe of Quraysh violated the treaty and attacked [2] the tribe of Bani Khuzāʿah, who were allies of the Muslims, and killed many of them.

The Conquest of Mecca

In the Ramadan of the 8th year A.H., shortly after the treaty was broken, Prophet Muḥammad (s) left Medina with ten thousand Muslims and headed towards Mecca to take the enemies by surprise. The Noble Prophet (s) made it very clear to the Muslims that they should avoid bloodshed at all costs, since starting bloodshed is not allowed near Masjid al-Ḥarām.

When they neared Mecca, the Prophet (s) sent a message to Quraysh telling them about how they could remain safe. In order to surrender, they could place their weapons on the ground, and then either remain in their houses, or seek refuge in the precincts of the Kaʿbah or the house of Abū Sufyān [3].

[1] 'Ali bin Ibrāhīm al-Qummi, The Exegesis of the Holy Qur'ān by al-Qummi
[2] The Prophet at that time had sent a group of Muslims to the frontiers of Syria to punish the Romans for attacking and killing unprotected Muslims. Although there were not many casualties, the Muslims did not return with the expected victory. Quraysh heard of this and thought that the Muslims had weakened militarily. Hence they took the opportunity to disturb the atmosphere of peace and tranquillity created by the treaty and attacked the Muslims.
[3] Abū Sufyān was the husband of Hind (who had eaten the liver of Ḥamzah). He accepted Islam out of fear during the Prophet's march to Mecca.

The Quraysh realized that they didn't have the means to defend themselves against an army of 10,000 Muslims. They also knew that the Prophet (s) was a trustworthy person who wouldn't go against his word. They surrendered, knowing that they would be safe if they did so.

When the Muslims entered Mecca, there were only a handful of the Quraysh who arrogantly wanted to resist the Muslims and attacked one of the groups. The Muslims defended themselves and some of the Quraysh who attacked were killed. Otherwise, the entry and the conquest of Mecca was peaceful. As soon as the Prophet entered into Masjid al-Ḥarām (wherein is the Ka'bah), he asked Imām ʿAlī (ʿa) to break the statues inside the Kaʿbah.

This proved to the Quraysh and idol worshippers that if the statues were gods they would have at least defended themselves, let alone protect their worshippers from the Muslims [1]. We can see from this event that the Prophet (s) spread Islam through its beauty and logic.

The Teachings of Prophet Muḥammad (ṣ)

Prophet Muḥammad (s) trained and guided people in two ways. He worked with many individuals and trained them, passing on to them the pure teachings of Islam that he embodied in 1:1 relationships. On the other hand he recognized the reality of how Islam needed a political order to attain its goals. Forming a government, establishing an army, and sending letters to other governments - all of these are indicative of his astute statesmanship.

His ten years of ruling from Medina are forever recorded in history as a shining example of government. When he passed away, 23 blessed years after the first revelation, he left behind a community at the peak of power and dignity. This same system and community, within a short span of time, became the most powerful force in the world.

Prophet Muḥammad (s) taught that a person should only submit to God; not to society, not to rulers, not to the majority; but only to God. He taught that absolute submission to God was the path to true freedom.

[1] Ayatullah Ja'far Subhani, The Message

In teaching freedom, he also taught us to avoid shameful sins. He urged us to be true to ourselves, our values and our ideals, rather than succumbing to sinful desires which were ultimately destructive. Once a person chooses the path of sin, they begin a journey of sometimes slow, but always inevitable, self-destruction and slavery to the devil and to one's own low desires.

Illness of the Prophet (ṣ)

The Prophet (s) had stated in Ghadīr Khumm that he would leave the world soon. He clearly stated that Imām ʿAlī (ʿa) is his rightful successor and all those at Ghadīr Khumm had witnessed and given their congratulatory statements and allegiance to Imām ʿAlī (ʿa). By 10 AH, Islam was firmly established and much could be gained by taking power and authority.

As the month of Muharram, marking the beginning of 11 AH, drew near, a letter reached Medina from Yamamah to the east. It was from a man, who had in fact earlier that year embraced Islam, claiming that he was now a partner in prophethood with the Prophet (s) and half of the Muslim domains should be given to him. His name was Musaylamah, famously known as Musaylamah al-Kadhāb, the liar. In Yemen, to the south, another false claimant arose by the name of Al-Aswad al-ʿAnsī. However, an even greater threat loomed to the north.

Because of the growing power of the Muslims, the Byzantine empire observed the events in the Arabian peninsula. In the years after hijrah, they clashed with the Muslim forces. To neutralize this grave threat upon his return to Medina, the Prophet (s) ordered an army to prepare themselves for war. He appointed Usāmah bin Zayd as the commander of the army. Usāmah was a young man, about twenty years old, whose father Zayd bin Ḥārithah had been killed by the Byzantines in the Battle of Muʾtah. Sadly, the day after the Prophet (s) appointed Usāmah to lead the Muslim army, our Noble Prophet (s) fell ill with a high fever and a headache.

Despite the Prophet's(s) illness, some among the Muslims objected and protested Usāmah's appointment. Efforts were also made to delay the army's departure. All this was done despite the Prophet's (s) constant insistence for the army to proceed.

This resistance to his commands disturbed the Prophet so much that at one point, he exclaimed so loudly that his voice could even be heard outside of the mosque, "O people! Mischief has been sparked off and rebellion has appeared like the pieces of a dark night. You have no excuse against me. I did not declare lawful anything except that which the Qur'ān declared lawful and did not declare unlawful anything except that which the Qur'ān declared unlawful." [1]

Tragically, the army never left al-Jurf where they had camped and the severity of the Prophet's (s) illness was even used as a further excuse to abandon the endeavour.

The Tragedy of Thursday

Despite the Prophet's (s) best efforts, the tragic events prior to his death did not end with only the matter of Usāmah's army. On the Thursday prior to his passing, while the senior commanders had come to inquire about the Prophet's (s) health he said to them, "Bring me a flat bone or a sheet and an ink-pot so that I may write something for you, after which you will never be misguided." [2]

However, at this critical moment ʿUmar ibn al-Khaṭṭāb said, "Sickness has overpowered the Prophet (s) and he is hallucinating. The Qur'ān is with you. The Divine Book is sufficient for us." [3]

Immediately others responded that the Prophet (s) must be obeyed and the argument became so heated that the Prophet (s) ordered everyone to leave. These calamitous events caused Ibn ʿAbbās to later comment, "The greatest calamity for Islam was that the discord and dispute of some companions prevented the Prophet (s) from writing the deed which he intended to write." [4]

[1] Sīreh Ibn Hishām, Vol. 2, P. 654; Ṭabaqāt Ibn Saʿd, Vol. 2, P. 216

[2] Al-Irshād, Vol. 1, P. 184; Ṣaḥīḥ al-Bukhārī, Vol. 4, P. 66; Ṣaḥīḥ Muslim, Vol. 5, P. 76

[3] Ṣaḥīḥ al-Bukhārī, Vol. 6, P. 9; Vol. 7, P. 120; Ṣaḥīḥ Muslim b-sharh al-Nawawī, Vol. 11, P. 90

[4] Sharh Nahj al-balāgha, Vol. 12, P. 20-21

Death of the Prophet

With the dawning of Monday, 28th of Safar, the world became bereft of the one whose birth heralded countless blessings, good tidings and guidance for all of mankind. The best man in creation left this realm. The most Noble Prophet (s), Muhammad ibn 'Abdullah (s) breathed his last while held in the arms of his brother, and true successor; ʿAlī ibn Abī Ṭālib (ʿa).

THE NOBLE QURAN

Section 4: The Word of the Almighty God

We have learnt that God has sent Prophets to guide humankind. Many of these prophets and messengers were given divine books to help guide their people. The Final Prophet and Messenger, Muhammad (s) was given the most perfect and advanced of these books: the Noble Qur'an.

The Noble Qur'an is the great miracle that God gave to Prophet Muhammad (s). As we have previously learned, the Noble Qurʾān was revealed by Allah (swt) to the Noble Prophet of Islam, Muḥammad (s). [1]

THE WORD OF THE ALMIGHTY

The Noble Qurʾān has come from Allah (swt). They are the exact words of God, sent through the Archangel Jibrāʾīl (ʿa) to our Noble Prophet Muhammad (s).

Thereafter, by the command of Allah (swt) of "Read (O Muḥammad)" {96:1}, the Noble Prophet (s) spoke these words to the people in the Arabic language, exactly as they were delivered to him by Jibrāʾīl (ʿa).

These words were memorised, written down, and compiled into a book during the Prophet's (s) life. The Qurʾān we have before us today is the same as the original Qurʾān that was compiled at the time of the Prophet (s). Every word, letter, and sentence is exactly the same.

[1] The main reference for this lesson is Sheikh Mansour Leghaei, eHAWZA Course: Sciences of the Qurʾān

PROVING THE MIRACULOUS NATURE OF THE QUR'ĀN

The Qur'ān is a miracle from Allah (swt) due to a number of reasons, including its unmatched eloquence.

The power and influence of language for the Arabs in the period before Islam is very important for us to understand why God Almighty gave the Noble Prophet (s) the Qur'ān as his miracle. Poets were highly respected members of society.

When the Prophet (s) spoke the Noble words of the Qur'ān, the beauty and eloquence of those words and their powerful meanings left most poets and the public amazed to the extent that some people claimed that the Noble Qur'ān was some kind of magic.

The Noble Qur'ān challenged the skilled Arab poets to produce even one chapter similar to the chapter of the Qur'ān in eloquence. This challenge was put forward multiple times. Of course, no one was able to meet such a challenge.

One simple example of the eloquence of the Qur'ān is the following āyah:

وَرَبَّكَ فَكَبِّرْ

"Magnify your Lord..." {74:3}

This āyah is very short- it contains two words and one preposition. The "wāw" in the beginning is there to indicate the beginning of the sentence. Then, looking at the two words that follow it, we see the following miracles of eloquence and language structure:

- It expresses such an important concept in just two words. On the other hand, the translation of this āyah in English requires many words to capture the true meaning: "Declare the greatness only [1] of your Lord."
- This phrase is a perfect palindrome. That means that it reads the same whether we read it backwards or forwards. This is very rare in literature, even when planned. Considering that the Prophet (s) was speaking this verbally, and not writing it or editing it, this makes it even more amazing.
- The wording has a rhythm and a melody to it.
- It flows with the rest of the surah which has many other short āyāt consisting of 2-3 words ending in the letter "rā'".
- Its content is perfectly in line with the rest of the Qur'ān and its detailed teachings on Tawhīd.
- Imagine trying to express the concept "Declare the greatness only of your Lord" in any language, in only two words, as a palindrome, on your first attempt, verbally, without knowing how to read or write, in a rhythmic way, consistent with the style of the chapter and the content of a long book, and without writing it or being able to edit it!

Proving the Authenticity of the Qur'ān

Authentic simply means: something true and therefore reliable. The Qur'ān is authentic and; the unchanged word of God throughout history.

All Muslims, despite their numerous differences of opinion on all sorts of topics in Islam, all believe in the same book. As much as different groups of Muslims may disagree on theological or historical issues, all refer to the same book, that is; the Noble Qur'ān, in the exact same form.

[1] The word "only" is understood from the verse by the placement of the direct object "Rabbaka" before the verb "Kabbir".

The Qur'ān has remained unchanged and this is why 1400 years after the Prophet (s) passed away, we still have only one copy of the Qur'ān, used by Muslims of all sects, nationalities and races. A Muslim in Indonesia, for example, will read from the exact same text of the Qur'ān as a Muslim in Turkey. Wherever in the world they are, Muslims have the same Qur'ān: the same sūrahs, āyāt, words, and letters. If you were to pick up a Qur'ān anywhere in the world right now, it would, without a doubt, be the same as all other copies of the Qur'ān.

If this were a book written by a human, it would be easy to change and alter, and there would have been different 'editions' or 'versions' of it. However, this is a Divine Book and protected from any change or alteration by Allah (swt), and thus remains unchanged till today. This is one of the miracles of the Qur'ān and one of the proofs for its being the Word of God.

إِنَّا نَحْنُ نَزَّلْنَا الذِّكْرَ وَإِنَّا لَهُ لَحَافِظُونَ

"Surely We have revealed the Reminder and We will most surely be its guardian." {9:15}

Recently, an ancient manuscript of fragments of the Noble Qur'ān kept at the university of Birmingham was dated using radiocarbon analysis. This dated the parchment on which the text was written to the period between AD 568 and AD 645 with 95.4% accuracy. The test was carried out in a laboratory at the University of Oxford. The result places the leaves close to the time of the Prophet Muḥammad (s), who lived between AD 570 and 632.

The Qur'ān is a Tightly Knit Book

The Noble Qur'ān refers to itself as 'Ḥakīm'. One meaning of this is 'wise'. Another meaning is that it is well-knit together. This means that the different parts of the Qur'ān complement each other, and never contradict one another. It also means that there are some miraculous aspects to the wording and structure of the Noble Qur'ān.

Let's look at one example of this. Usually we speak about "doing" good or evil actions. Similarly, the Noble Qur'ān uses this common expression of "doing" an action with the term "'amal" many times. However, in some particular instances the Qur'ān will use the word "kasab" when referring to evil actions. The word "kasab" refers to having done an action so frequently that it has become a part of the character of a person. So when Allah (swt) speaks about who deserves to enter the Hellfire, the word "kasab" (earned / attained) is used rather than the word "did" ('amal). An example of this is in the following āyah:

بَلَىٰ مَن كَسَبَ سَيِّئَةً وَأَحَٰطَتْ بِهِۦ خَطِيٓـَٔتُهُۥ فَأُو۟لَٰٓئِكَ أَصْحَٰبُ ٱلنَّارِ ۖ هُمْ فِيهَا خَٰلِدُونَ

"Certainly whoever earns misdeeds and is besieged by his sinfulness—such shall be the inmates of the Fire, and they will remain in it [forever]." {2:81}

By using the word "kasab", the Qur'ān

- Firstly emphasizes that the ones who deserve the Hell-fire are those who repeatedly do an evil action until it becomes part of their personality.
- Secondly avoids contradiction in other places of the Qur'ān where Allah (swt) states that those who do evil deeds may be forgiven and enter Paradise.

There are many examples of such precise choice of wording in the Noble Qur'ān. How could a human, who verbally spoke these words over a span of 23 years remember what word he had used in one place, and maintain or change their wording so that it remains consistent with the message without contradictions? Surely, this is beyond the abilities of any human and proves that this book is the word of God.

Āyah and Sūrah

The Noble Qur'ān consists of āyah (plural: āyāt) and sūrah (plural: suwar)

Āyah: This is often translated as verse. However, this is not the most accurate translation for the word āyah. Āyah literally means 'sign'. Each āyah of the Qur'ān is a sign of:

- The unmatchable eloquence of the Qur'ān, as no one could even replicate a single āyah of the Qur'ān
- The greatness of Allah (swt), the author of that āyah

Sūrah: This is often translated as a chapter. However, this is not the best translation for a sūrah. Literally, Sūrah comes from "sūr" which is a wall built around a city to contain and fortify it. Every Sūrah is like the walls around a city that bring together and contain the āyāt within it. Just like cities are made up of different things that function very well together (houses, schools, hospitals etc...) similarly a sūrah of the Qur'ān will often discuss different themes such as theology, rules of practical life, and history. Even though the themes are different, they complement one another just like the different parts of a city complement each other.

Just like some cities share similarities but are different in other ways, we see some sūrahs share similarities and remind us of other sūrahs, but are also unique and different in their own way.

When we are reading the Qur'ān, we should take time to reflect and contemplate on the relationship between the āyāt and themes within each sūrah as this can help us gain more meaning from the Holy Qur'ān.

The Qur'ān Guides the Intellect

As mentioned above, it is imperative to reflect on the relationship of the āyāt and themes found within the Qur'ān. The Noble Qur'ān repeatedly encourages us to use our intellect when it comes to our beliefs about the world we live in and the decisions that we make in our life

THE MIRACLES OF THE NOBLE QURAN*

In the previous section, we discussed the authenticity of the Noble Qur'ān. We discussed that the Qur'ān is the word of God and that there are a number of proofs for this. We discussed that the Qur'ān:

- is unmatchable in its eloquence
- is unchanged since its revelation
- is unique in its style and expressions
- is tightly knit together and does not contradict itself

In this lesson, we will discuss some further proofs which are secondary to the main proofs but are very interesting.

Scientific Miracles of the Noble Qur'ān

Even though the goal of the Noble Qur'ān is not to present intricate scientific details, at times, it presents information about the reality of the world that was only discovered by humans in the last 100 years or so. If these scientific facts were not known to any humans at the time of Prophet Muhammad (s), where did this knowledge come from? It must be that it came from Allah (swt) who revealed this information in the Qur'ān, as another miracle of the Qur'ān for people who would come at a later time. We will look at some of these examples here:

Expansion of the Universe

"And it is We Who have constructed the heaven with might, and verily, it is We Who are steadily expanding it." {51:47}

For a very long time, scientists and thinkers thought of the universe as constant in nature, meaning that it is always the same in size, and that it has always been around and had no beginning.

*The main reference for this lesson was: Sheikh Mansour Leghaei, eHAWZA Course: Sciences of the Qur'ān

However, by the beginning of the 1900s, famous scientists such as the Russian physicist Alexander Friedmann, the Belgian cosmologist Georges Lemaitre, the pn American astronomer Edwin Hubble, and the German-born Albert Einstein, all had seemingly proved, in one way or another, that the universe was continuously expanding.

Amazingly, we have a passage in the Qur'ān which refers to this phenomenon. This is incredible, considering that the Qur'ān was revealed at a time when telescopes and such advanced scientific understanding were not even close to being invented or thought of.

The Creation of Human Beings from Water

> "Allah has created every moving (living) creature from water..." {24:45}

It is commonly believed in modern science that water is the main component of organic (living) matter. Furthermore, it is accepted that 50-90% of living things consist of water. Simply put, without water, we cannot think of life. Today, astronauts send space probes to other planets in space such as Mars to search for any signs of water. This is because they know that if water is present, then life is possible. So it is said that water is the precursor to life, and hence this could be another meaning for the verse from the Qur'ān mentioned above.The fact that this scientific information, which has only been found out very recently, was in the Qur'ān 1400 years ago, indicates that the Qur'ān is not the word of a man, but the Word of God.

Iron Sent Down

Surah al-Ḥadīd makes reference to iron being "sent down." [57:25] This may at first seem strange as it appears to speak about iron being "sent" to Earth rather than being "in the Earth." However, we have recently come to learn that at least some of the iron on Earth came from meteorites [1] and that iron was in fact "sent down" to Earth from space.

[1] Chase, M. (2019, March 2). What is the origin of iron? Sciencing. Retrieved December 30, 2022, from https://sciencing.com/origin-iron-5371252.html

PROPHECIES IN THE NOBLE QUR'ĀN

There are various predictions made that the Noble Qur'ān accurately made future events and have now taken place. We mention a few here:

The Victory of the Romans

"The Romans have been defeated. In the nearer land, and they, after their defeat, will be victorious. Within a few [three to nine] years. The decision of the matter, before and after (these events) is only with Allah..." {30:2-4}

According to historians, these words were revealed around 620 A.H., almost 7 years after the idol-worshipping Persian Empire had severely defeated the Christian Roman army in 613-14 A.H. In fact, the Roman Empire (Byzantium) was defeated so badly that it seemed that the empire was on the verge of collapse. No one really thought it would ever become victorious again.During this time though, the above words were revealed, declaring that the Roman Empire will be victorious again in some (which in Arabic typically refers to 3 to 9) years. The Arab polytheists found this impossible to believe. However, of course, this is exactly what occurred. The Romans fought the Persians again a few years later and were victorious.

The Exploration of Space

"O company of jinn and human beings. If you are able to pierce through the confines of the heavens and Earth, pierce through them. You will not pierce through, except with clear authority." {55:33}

Here, one application of the verse could be to the exploration of space by human beings, which only began in the late 1950s. The first man in space was a Russian pn astronaut named Yuri Gagarin.

The Arabic word sultān, translated here as "clear authority" has other meanings as well, including force and power. It has been suggested that here is the great power or energy contained within flying objects that are launched into space.

CONCLUSION

Besides the unmatchable eloquence and unique style of the Holy Qur'ān, there are also other arguments that help to demonstrate that the Qur'ān is the authentic Word of God. These include some of the scientific miracles in the Qur'ān as well as the prophecies made in the Qur'ān which later came to be true.

A COMPARISON OF MUSLIM AND CHRISTIAN BELIEFS

Section 5

Prophet ʿĪsā (ʿa) and Lady Maryam (ʿa)

The Noble Qurʾān states the true story of Prophet ʿĪsā and is the only real source about the life of this great Messenger and Prophet.The Bible and other historians do not give a true version of the story. We know that the Bible has been changed many times over the course of history, starting immediately after Prophet ʿĪsā left his people. Within the Bible, there is no real evidence pointing towards the truth of the story as there are no accounts from witnesses, letters to reference, or revelation from other Prophets to indicate any truth. Islam is the only non-Christian religion that acknowledges Prophet ʿĪsā (ʿa). We believe in him as an immaculate messenger of God. Muslims also believe in the great status of Lady Maryam and that Prophet Īsā (ʿa) is alive and will return to earth along with Imām al-Mahdī (ʿaj).

The Truth about Lady Maryam (ʿa)

Perhaps due to the miraculous nature of the birth of Prophet Īsā (ʿa), there are many accusations against Lady Maryam:

- The Jews accuse her of not being a chaste woman and that she had a child through adultery
- Some Christians- Catholics and Orthodox Christians-say that she was 'the mother of god'-although even in the Bible this title is not given to her.
- Other Christians-mainly Protestants and Presbyterians -do not give any significance to Lady Maryam and she has no role in their theology, nor do they acknowledge the concept of the "Immaculate Conception."

The Noble Qurʾān mentions her by name twenty-five times including being mentioned as Prophet ʿĪsā's mother sixteen times. This is to emphasize and leave no doubt that Prophet ʿĪsā (ʿa) is not the son of God and also to show that Lady Maryam is not the mother of god.

The Noble Qurʾān also mentions that Prophet ʿĪsā (ʿa) and Lady Maryam were both worshipping God, and ate and drank, which proves it impossible for them to be deities.

"O Jesus, son of Mary, did you say to people worship me and my mother as two gods besides Allah (swt)? Jesus says: 'Glory be to You, I would not say what I do not have a right to say, I only said what You commanded me to say..." {5:116}

As mentioned, Lady Maryam is praised often in the Noble Qur'ān and in the narrations of the Ahl al-Bayt(ʿa). Some of her many virtues are as follows:

1. She is one of the four best women in history. It is narrated from the Prophet of Islam (s): "Verily, Allah(swt) has chosen from among women four ladies: Àsiyah, the daughter of Mezaîim, the wife of Pharaoh; Maryam the mother of ʿĪsā (ʿa) ; Khadījah the daughter of Khuwaylid, and Fātimah (ʿa)the daughter of the Prophet Muhammad (s) who is the most honorable of them all."
2. She is the only lady whose name is explicitly mentioned in the Qur'ān.
3. She is the first woman to be 'chosen' by Allah (swt).
4. She was a woman who was spoken to by angels.
5. She has the right of intercession.

The Life of Lady Maryam (ʿa)

Lady Maryam's father was Prophet Imrān (ʿa) and her mother's name was Hannah. Her mother had a sister called Elizabeth, who was married to Prophet Zakarriyā (ʿa).

Both these sisters were tested with the hardship of not being able to have children. Hanna and Prophet Imrān (ʿa) both prayed for a child sincerely and Hanna vowed that if she had a child, she would dedicate him to the service of Allah (swt). Her husband had a dream that a boy would be born into his family, and so they assumed that the child was the boy. However, before Lady Maryam (ʿa) was born, her father passed away.

When Hanna gave birth, she had a daughter, Lady Maryam, and not the boy they had assumed the baby would be from the dream. She was shocked, but since she was a faithful woman, she kept her vow. As soon as she was old enough, Hanna left Lady Maryam to serve Allah (swt) in a temple. The men of the temple drew lots to see who should look after Lady Maryam (ʿa), and Prophet Zakariyyā (ʿa) was the one who was selected to look after her.

As Lady Maryam spent her life in the worship of Allah (swt), He would send her sustenance miraculously; she would have the fruits of winter in the summer and the fruits of summer in the winter. One day, Lady Maryam was visited by Jabrā'īl and was given the good news of a child, called ʿĪsā (ʿa).

Birth of Prophet ʿĪsā (a)

Jabrāʾīl gave glad tidings to Lady Maryam of having a son who would be a Prophet. pn However, Lady Maryam was not married and this caused her a lot of worry. Jabrāʾīl said to her that Allah (swt) had willed this and so it would happen. One night, she was visited by Jabrāʾīl, but in the form of a man. She sought refuge with Allah (swt), but then realized the man was an angel giving her the message of glad tidings and that she would have a son.

Lady Maryam (ʿa) left her town to have her baby but once she came back with her son, the accusations began. Instructed to observe a vow of silence, Lady Maryam (ʿa) responded by pointing to her baby, Prophet ʿĪsā (ʿa). The people began to condemn her, but suddenly Prophet ʿĪsā (ʿa) began to speak.

"He said: I am the devotee of Allah (swt). He has given me the Scripture and has made a Prophet, and made me blessed wherever I am..." {19:30}

The Book of Prophet ʿĪsā (ʿa)

The Noble Qur'ān definitely confirms that a book called the Injīl was revealed to Prophet ʿĪsā (ʿa). However, we have to question if this is the same Bible that exists today.

Did Prophet ʿĪsā (ʿa) Have a Book That He Taught?

The Noble Qur'ān confirms that Prophet ʿĪsā (ʿa) had a book revealed to him and this was called the Injīl. It seems from the present Bible that Jesus had a Scripture called 'the Gospel'. Christians however, do not recognize any written Gospel for Jesus. They claim he did not consign to writing his own teachings and directed his apostles not to write, but to preach the Gospel verbally to other people. In justification of their belief, they offer a literal interpretation for the above mentioned Biblical quotations. Thus, they assert the term 'Gospel' in those passages has a literal meaning, i.e. glad tiding.

This claim is an attempt to conceal a historical fact about the original Gospel. Unfortunately, the Gospel of Jesus was lost or destroyed by the Jews. It is expressed by a number of historians that divisions between early sects of Christianity also encouraged the destruction of writings of which they did not approve.

Who Wrote the Gospels?

The Bible that we have with us today consists of the Old Testament and the New Testament. The New Testament contains the 'four gospels' and a remaining section called the 'Letters of Paul'. Sometime after the passing away of Prophet ʿĪsā (ʿa), many people began to write 'gospels'. Between 50 to 100 gospels were written, and the council of the time chose 4 to be in the current New Testament: the gospels of Mathew, Mark, Luke and John.

All Christian scholars agree that the writers of these gospels were not the disciples of Jesus (ʿa). The Bible was written by four people who did not have direct access to Prophet ʿĪsā (ʿa). They were not his companions or successors nor were they messengers. They did not hear these words from Prophet ʿĪsā (ʿa) and write them down exactly, however, Mark was one of the students of St. Peter, who was one of the disciples.

The Gospels also differ in many instances from the narration of the genealogy and the birth of Jesus to his so-called crucifixion.

It is evident from the chronology of events that the current Bible that the Christians have today is not the book of Prophet ʿĪsā (ʿa). It is not the Injīl mentioned in the Noble Qurʾān. While the original source of some of the material may be the original holy book, we cannot rely on these gospels because they are not the words of God or the words of Jesus (ʿa). Rather, they were written by others later.

All this shows the miracle of the Noble Qurʾān. It demonstrates the blessings that Muslims have in being able to access a true Noble Book which is the word of Allah revealed directly to His Messenger (s), compiled during his life, in its original language, and being preserved until today, more than 1400 years after it was revealed. We are truly lucky as Muslims to have direct access to the words of God as revealed onto the heart of Prophet Muḥammad (s), and we should be abundantly grateful for this miraculous blessing.

The Myth of Crucifixion

Christians believe that Prophet ʿĪsā (ʿa) was crucified and died on the cross. Crucifixion was a form of torture, done by hanging someone on the cross. They also believe, depending on sect, that he was resurrected and raised to heaven by Allah (swt). According to the Noble Qurʾān, however, Prophet ʿĪsā (ʿa) was never crucified; he was raised up to heaven by Allah (swt) without being caught by his enemies. The Noble Qur'ān emphasizes the fact that Prophet ʿĪsā (ʿa) was not crucified.

"And because of their saying: We killed Messiah, Jesus; son of Mary, the Messenger of Allah, but they killed him not, nor crucified him, but it appeared so to them, and those who differ therein are full of doubts. They have no (certain) knowledge, they follow nothing but conjecture. For, surely they killed him not. But Allah raised him up unto Himself. And Allah is Ever All-Powerful, All-Wise." {4:157-158}

An authentic narration from Imam al-Bāqir (ʿa) clarifies what really happened. "Verily, on the night that Allah (swt) had promised to raise Jesus (ʿa) to Him, Jesus (ʿa) invited his disciples, who were twelve men, to a house. Jesus (ʿa) came out to them from a corner of the house whilst he was drying his head from water. He then said: Surely, Allah (swt) revealed to me that He will raise me this time to Him and will clear me from the Jews, so which one of you is willing to have my image cast upon him to be killed and crucified and he will be with me in the hereafter? A young man from among them said: I (will accept) Oh Rūḥullāh! Jesus (ʿa) replied: So, you will be the one."[1]

Christians believe that all humans are sinful, and that Prophet ʿĪsā (ʿa) dying on the cross saves all humans from their sinfulness if they believe in Christianity. This is why the Noble Qurʾān, especially in Sūrah al-Nisāʾ, Allah (swt) emphasizes so many times that the crucifixion did not happen, and Prophet ʿĪsā (ʿa) did not die.
Furthermore, it is false to claim that one person suffering and dying leads to the sins of other people being forgiven. It is also a false claim that all people are born sinful and are prone to being punished. This is because Allah (swt) is Just. He would not punish a person or cause him to be born sinful when that person has not done anything wrong. He would also not cause a person to suffer in order to forgive the sins of another, or forgive a person because of the suffering of another. All this would be against the Justice of Allah (swt), and logic necessitates that God is Just.

[1] ʿAlī ibn Ibrāhīm al-Qummī, Tafsīr al-Qummī, Vol.1 P.111.

Did Prophet ʿĪsā (ʿa) Ever Claim to Be God?

The Noble Qur'ān states that on the Day of Judgment, Allah (swt) will ask Prophet ʿĪsā (ʿa) if he asked people to either worship him or his mother. The purpose of this rhetorical question is for the Christians to hear from Prophet ʿĪsā (ʿa) that he never had such a blasphemous claim.

"And when Allah (swt) will say: Oh Jesus son of Mary! Did you say unto men: Worship me and my mother as two gods besides Allah (swt)? He will say: Glory be to You! It was not for me to say what I had no right to say, Had it said such a thing, You would surely have known it. You know what is in my inner-self though I do not know what is in Yours; truly, You only You, are the All-Knower of all that is hidden." {5:116} Nowhere even in the present gospels does it indicate that Jesus ever explicitly claimed to be God. The Encyclopedia Britannica states: "Neither the word Trinity, nor the explicit doctrine as such, appears in the New Testament, nor did Jesus and his followers intend to contradict the Shema in the Old Testament: Hear, Oh Israel: The Lord our God is one Lord. {Deuteronomy, 6:4}

The worship of God was always focal in Prophet ʿĪsā's (ʿa) (ʿa) life. For instance, when his disciples asked him to teach them how to pray (Luke 11:1-2) he taught them to pray to God; the Father, not to himself. Notice that the words "Father! Grant us" indicate that included himself among the creation of God, acknowledging a high authority; 'God' over all of them. Similarly, according to John, Jesus said to Mary Magdalene: "I am going to ascend to my father and your father, to my God and your God." {Gospel of John, 20:17}

According to Mark, Jesus even did not allow himself to be called 'good' let alone 'God'. Mark narrates that as Jesus was setting out on a journey, a man ran up and knelt before him, and asked him: "Good teacher. What must I do to inherit eternal life?" Jesus said to him, "Why do you call me good? No one is good but God alone." {Gospel of Mark, 10:17-18}

We conclude from these discussions that all the rational and textual evidence indicates that Prophet ʿĪsā (ʿa) is not God. In a debate between Imām ar-Riḍā (ʿa) and Jathaliq, the head of the Christians at Maʾmūn's palace, Imām ar-Riḍā (ʿa) uses a reasoning saying if Jesus is God, then he should not be praying. Jathaliq admits the fact about Jesus praying and fasting and in turn Imām (ʿa) asks, "Then to whom is he praying? [1]

Extension: Sections 5.2 and 5.3 include further Discussions on the Beliefs in Trinity and Crucifixion. This section is for readers who are from a Christian background and who may be interested in a more detailed discussion on the beliefs in Trinity and Crucifixion.

[1] Shaykh Ṣadūq, Uyun Akhbar al-Rida, Vol. 1, P. 159.

5.2- The Doctrine of Trinity

THE TRINITY

The doctrine of Trinity is the central doctrine in Christian theology. It is the belief in a Triune Godhead, that God is 'three in one'. The trinity consists of God the Father, the Son, and the Holy Spirit. It also includes the belief that God became incarnate in Jesus and that Jesus (the Son) is of the same substance as the Father.

Historical development of the doctrine and how it was influenced by external sources

The doctrine of Trinity cannot be understood completely without an appreciation of the historical development of the doctrine of Trinity. Firstly, we must note it is not mentioned anywhere in the Bible itself. In the period immediately following the life of Jesus Christ on earth, there were many questions about his identity, his status and the claim of incarnation. The more the Church claimed that Jesus was God incarnate, the more need there was to explain the relationship of Jesus Christ to God. The roots of the doctrine of Trinity lie here.

It took until the middle of the fourth century for there to be any sort of consensus on this issue. Tertullian introduced the terminology of Trinity in the last second or early third century, but it was after this that the Arian controversy came about, forcing the Church to formalise its belief about the significance of Jesus. Arius (c.250-c.336) was a priest in one of the major churches in Alexandria. He taught that the Father and the Son do not have the same essence, that the Son is a created being, and that there was a time when the Son did not exist. Thus Arius taught that Jesus was 'the first among creatures', but not divine in any meaningful way.

Athanasius (c. 297-c. 373) was another Alexandrian priest who strongly opposed Arius' teachings, and claimed Jesus to be divine. This controversy divided the Church, and it had to be settled. The Emperor Constantine the Great convened a council of bishops in order to come to an answer to settle this controversy, an answer which would then become official Church doctrine. The Council voted in favour of the view of Athanasius, and the doctrine that the Son and the Father were of the same substance became official Church teaching.

It is important to note that most bishops were not in agreement with either Athanasius or Arius. However, Athanasius managed to exert his influence over many of the delegates, and so all but two signed his Creed. Arius, and two others, refused to do, and were later excommunicated.

Internal Evidence from the Bible itself that contradicts the divinity of Jesus

There are a number of Biblical passages that clearly contradict the doctrine of Trinity. Some of them are listed below:

- These passages indicate God cannot be seen or heard, so can Jesus (who was seen and heard) be God?
- "And the Father who sent me has himself borne witness about me. His voice you have never heard, his form you have never seen," {John 5:37}.
- "No man hath seen God at any time" {John 1:18}
- In his letter to the Colossians, Paul says: "And He is the image of the invisible God, the first-born of all creation." {Colossians 1:15-21}
- Jesus is related to have prayed in the following passage, if he is God, then to whom does he pray?
- "And after he had dismissed the crowds, he went up on the mountain by himself to pray." {Matthew 14:23}
- Here, Jesus is described clearly as a prophet, not as the son of God;
- When Jesus entered Jerusalem, the whole city was stirred and asked, "Who is this?" The crowds answered, "This is Jesus, the prophet from Nazareth in Galilee." {Matthew 21:10-11}
- "...... Then Jesus told them, "A prophet is honoured everywhere except in his own hometown..." {Matthew 13:57}

- "What things?" he asked. "About Jesus of Nazareth," they replied. "He was a prophet, powerful in word and deed before God and all the people." {Luke 24:19}
- "And this is eternal life, that they know you the only true God, and Jesus Christ whom you have sent." {John 17:3}
- Here, he is described as someone needing God's approval and being dependent on God:
- "Ye men of Israel, hear these words; Jesus of Nazareth, a man approved of God among you by miracles and wonders and signs, which God did by him." {Acts 2:22}
- "For I have come down from heaven, not to do my own will but the will of him who sent me." {John 6:38}
- The following passages clearly indicate there is only One God, which is the main point we want to prove:
- "You were shown these things so that you might know that the Lord is God; besides him there is no other." {Deuteronomy 4:35}
- "I am the LORD, and there is no other, besides me there is no God; I equip you," {Isaiah 45:5}
- When Jesus was asked about the greatest commandment of all, he quoted this verse: "Hear, oh Israel, the Lord is our God, the Lord is One." {Deuteronomy 6:4}

We can see from the above passages that the Bible in many places indicates that God is one. However, Christians argue that God is one but in a plurality. They argue that the word "one" or in Hebrew (Ehad) is not one alone but one as a compound unity. And they will quote this passage: "Therefore a man shall leave his father and his mother and hold fast to his wife, and they shall become one flesh." {Genesis 2:24} or {Ephesians 5:31}. Yet in fact, the word "Ehad" in Hebrew could mean one as alone and one as a compound unity, depending on its context. For example: "one person who has no other, either son or brother" {Ecclesiastes 4:8}

Christians may also quote this passage in the first book of the bible, and say this shows that god is more than one. "Then God said, "Let us make man in our image, after our likeness..." {Genesis 1:26}. However, that is the 'magestic we', used to indicate status and respect, not an actual plurality.

If we look in the Bible, we can see other verses that clearly used the word one or 'Ehad' to indicate a singular one, not a compound unity. Some examples follow:

- "Look to Abraham your father and to Sarah who bore you; for he was but one when I called him, that I might bless him and multiply him." {Isaiah 51:2}
- "See now that I, even I, am he, and there is no god beside me" {Deuteronomy 32:39}
- The first commandment that Moses taught the Israelites says: "I am the LORD your God, who brought you out of the land of Egypt, out of the house of bondage. You shall have no other gods before Me" {Exodus 20:2-3}.

Christians may also refer to the following passage to try to prove the divinity of Jesus: "I and the Father are one." {John 10:30}

This may seem to indicate some sort of unity between God and Jesus, but when we look at the quote in context, we see that it is not claiming divinity for Jesus: "I give them eternal life, and they shall never perish; no one will snatch them out of my hand. My Father, who has given them to me, is greater than all; no one can snatch them out of my Father's hand. I and the Father are one."

The passage is indicating that the Father and Jesus are one in seeing that if the person accepts faith, they shall remain in faith. It is referring to a unity of purpose, not a unity of substance. It is this same unity of purpose which is referred to in the following passage: "...Holy Father, keep them in your name, which you have given me, that they may be one, even as we are one." {John 17:11}

Jesus here is using the same word "one" for himself and for his disciples. Does that mean that his disciples are one in substance with him and with God? Of course not! He means his disciples should unify in one and same purpose.

So we can see that there is very little evidence within the Bible for the belief in Trinity, and in fact there is plenty of evidence for a belief in a true Unity of God.

Trinity Contradicts Logic

If we read the first passage of the Gospel of John: "In the beginning was the Word, and the Word was with God, and the Word was God." (John 1:1), we see it contains a clear logical contradiction. How can the Word be 'with God' (i.e. separate to God) and yet be God at the same time? In fact, this particular quote, was plagiarised by the writer of "The Gospel According to John", who borrowed it from a Greek philosopher named Philo.

If we read verse 14 from the same chapter it says: "The Word became flesh and made his dwelling among us" (John 1:14), we can clearly see that this verse implies that god has changed from the unlimited spiritual nature into humanly flesh nature. This fact of God changing his nature is rejected by God, in his own words according to the Bible itself: "I am the LORD, and I do not change." (Malachi 3:6). If God can change, it means he can be updated, or created into a different form or new shape that he wasn't like before, which implies that he needs that form or space to exist, and God cannot be dependent on anything. This shows that God the Son is not co-equal to God the Father and God the Holy Spirit, as he had to undergo change, and they (the Father and presumably the Holy Spirit) did not.

God's Omnipotence

Christians typically ask, If God is omnipotent, (All Powerful) shouldn't he be able to take on a human form and dwell among humans and behave like humans? If not, how can such a being be called all-powerful?

From a logical point of view, the question itself is illogical and an example of fallacy. It is similar to the question: "Can God create a rock so heavy that He can't lift it Himself". The problem is it contains a self-contradiction, mainly, that God is all-powerful and not-all-powerful at the same time. The question works grammatically but not intellectually.

When we say God is omnipotent, we mean He has power over all things which have an intellectual existence. However, possibilities like the above do not have a real intellectual existence, we cannot even imagine them! Therefore, they fall into the realm of non-existence and thus have nothing to do with God's Omnipotence.

A Challenge to Christians

We found nowhere in the bible where Jesus says: "I am God" or where Jesus says: "Worship Me". Can Christians present real evidence from their own book that Jesus is divine or should be worshipped?

The most a Christian may claim is by referring to the following passage: "For there are three that bear record in heaven, the Father, the Word [Jesus], and the Holy Ghost: and these three are one." (I John 5: 7) KJV.

Note that this verse is only found in the King James Version. Almost all modern versions of the bibles do not include that particular verse anymore! It was removed and declared a fabrication. Even though this verse played such an important role in the faith and the prayers of Christians, it is no longer considered part of the Bible. Instead, the following versions of the verse are now found in different versions of the Bible:

- "For there are three that testify: the Spirit, the water and the blood; and the three are in agreement." (I John 5: 7) NIV.
- "For there are three that testify: the Spirit and the water and the blood; and these three agree." (I John 5: 7) ESV.

CONCLUSION

In this lesson, we have analysed the doctrine of Trinity. We have come to a number of conclusions:

- 'Trinity' is not mentioned in the Bible itself. It developed over four centuries after the ascension of Jesus (as)
- Trinity is illogical
- There is no sound evidence for the doctrine of Trinity in the Bible
- There is plenty of evidence contradicting the doctrine of Trinity within the Bible

5.3- The Doctrine of Crucifixion

Another of the main Christian doctrines is that of Crucifixion and salvation. Christians believe that Jesus was captured by the Jews of his time, nailed to the cross and tortured, until he died. They believe he was resurrected three days later and came back to Earth as a final miracle.

The claimed event of crucifixion is central to Christian theology. They believe that all humans are born sinful, because of the 'original sin' of Adam. They believe the only way for our sins to be expiated is for god himself to suffer for them, and they see the crucifixion of Jesus as god suffering in for us to be freed from sin and achieve salvation. We read in Paul's First letter to the Corinthians, "And if Christ is not risen from the dead, then our preaching is vain, and your faith is also in vain. More than that, and we are then found to be false witnesses of God ..." {1 Corinthians 15:14-15}

The Doctrine of Salvation is Illogical

The doctrine of salvation as presented in Christianity is illogical. It is against God's justice that all humans should suffer and be born with an inclination towards sin, simply because one human, Adam, made a mistake. The justice of god rejects the idea that he can punish innocent people for the sins of the others, as we can see it clearly in the book of Ezekiel in the Old Testament. "The one who sins is the one who will die. The child will not share the guilt of the parent, nor will the parent share the guilt of the child. The righteousness of the righteous will be credited to them, and the wickedness of the wicked will be charged against them." {Ezekiel 18:20}. We also see this reference to the justice of God in the following passage: "I the Lord search the heart, and examine the mind, to reward each person according to their conduct, according to what their deeds deserve." {Jeremiah 17:10}.

The Holy Qur'an further confirms this idea:

"And no bearer of burdens will bear the burden of another" (35:18)

So we see that this doctrine goes against justice, and this ethical argument is supported by Biblical evidence.

Biblical Passages Contradicting The Doctrine of Salvation

We also find numerous passages in the Bible that contradict that dogma of the inheritance of the Original Sin, Crucifixion, and Resurrection.

- Jesus was baptised by John the Baptist (Prophet YaÎyÁ) as we are told in {Matthew 3:13-17}. This would imply that that Jesus was regarded as a sinner, who has inherited the original sin. How can he then be the vehicle for salvation?
- The following passage indicates that God does not want sacrifice in exchange for atonement of sins. Yet Christians claim that the sacrifice of Jesus was necessary for the atonement of sin.
- "For I desire mercy, not sacrifice, and acknowledgment of God rather than burnt offerings." {Hosea 6:6}
- If we read {Luke 23:26-34} we can clearly see that the person who was crucified could actually be Simon of Cyrene, and certainly not Jesus.

Contradictions within the Biblical Narrations of the story

The story of crucifixion has many discrepancies and contradictions, if we compare the accounts across the Four Gospels.

- What day did Jesus die? That is a very simple question! We are told in both Mark and John. In Mark, we are told that it is the day after the Passover meal was eaten in Jerusalem. {Mark 14:12-16}. And In John, we are told that it is the day before the Passover meal was eaten, on the day of preparation for the Passover {John 19:14}. And many more. Conclusion: these accounts are full of discrepancies and they are not reliable.
- What were Jesus' last words? Mark and Matthew state they were: "My God, my God, why have you forsaken me?" John states that they were: "It is finished", while Luke states they were: "Father, into your hands I commit my spirit."

There are many other contradictions within the Biblical narrations of this story, indicating that this story may not have a true origin.

Biblical verses that Reject the Crucifixion

Here, we would like to explore one important point in greater detail: did the historical event claimed by Christians- that Jesus of Nazareth, son of Mary, was crucified by the soldiers of Pontius Pilate- really occur?

The intention of this argument is not to prove that a crucifixion did not take place but rather that it was not Jesus of Nazareth who was crucified. The early Christians had doubt about this.

The Holy Qur'an rejects that Jesus was ever crucified and killed. This rejection is very much justified, because of the reasons below:

- We have no first-hand accounts of the event. The only sources we have are the accounts of Josephus, a Jewish historian, and Tacitus, a Roman historian, both of whom were not present at the time of the crucifixion.
- The Jewish Talmud tells us that Jesus was stoned to death. This contradicts the Biblical account (of course neither account is true)
- Early Christian sources: there are significant early sources that all suggests that were Christian groups that did not believe in the crucifixion and rejected that concept, or at least questions how the crucifixion took place

Biblical verses that Reject the Crucifixion

- **The Writings of the Early Church Fathers.** Such as have Ignasous , Polycarp, Justin, Uranaiuos, Tulian and Hepolaias. These fathers were attacking the groups who did believe in Crucifixion, indicating there were such groups. Perhaps most known among them was a group in Egypt called the Missillidions, who believed it was a person by the name of Simon of Cyrene who was in fact crucified.
- **The New Testament Apocryphal Books.** Such as books of Jeeuo which go back to the third century in Egypt, says that Jesus was not crucified. The Apocrypha of Peter and the Acts of John are early books that were canonised but which state that Jesus was not crucified.

- **The New Testament itself.** When Jesus was arrested and brought back to Pontius Pilate, the Roman Governor of Judea, we are told in Matthew that Pilate really did not want to do anything to Jesus. He asked the crowd to choose between freeing Jesus or freeing another prisoner, and that he would allow this as a gesture of mercy: "so when the crowd gathered, Pilate asked them, "Which one do you want me to release to you, Jesus Barabbas or Jesus, who is called the Messiah" {Matthew: 27:16, NIV}. The people chose Barabbas and then Jesus was crucified. However in the New Revised Standard Version of the Bible said that the two persons were "Jesus the Barabbas" and the other was "Jesus the Messiah" This is further clarified in the following passage: "At that time they had a well-known prisoner whose name was Jesus Barabbas." {Matthew 27:16} NIV.

So who was set free? Jesus of Nazareth or another man named Jesus?
It seems that it was Jesus of Nazareth who was set free. This is because the name "Barabbas" literally means 'son of the Father'. Of course, this would be referring to Jesus of Nazareth, and so if it is Barabbas who was set free, then it is Jesus of Nazareth who was set free, and another man, also named Jesus, who was instead crucified.

This may explain why the Coptic Christian Church canonized Pilate as a saint! Do you justify sainthood for the man who killed Jesus? Or for the man who saved him and set him free?

There is another issue to consider here. There is a variant in several Greek manuscripts of the Gospel of Matthew. The traditional text of Matthew 27:16-17 reads as follows in the New American Standard Bible (NASB): "At that time they were holding a notorious prisoner, called Barabbas. So when they the people gathered together, Pilate said to them, "Whom do you want me to release for you? Barabbas, or Jesus who is called Christ?" Several manuscripts, however, name the criminal "Jesus Barabbas" and have Pilate ask:

"Whom do you want me to release for you, Jesus Barabbas or Jesus who is called the Messiah? "(v. 17). Many textual scholars believe the double name "Jesus Barabbas" was the original reading. They suggest that "Jesus" was omitted from several Greek manuscripts of Matthew out of reverence.

This shows us that the criminal being held along with Jesus of Nazareth was also named Jesus (Barabbas), and that he may have been the one actually crucified, but that this was later historically confused with Jesus of Nazareth, the Messiah. It also seems from some account that Jesus Barabbas was claiming to the king of the Jews, and we see in many places in the Bible that the person who was crucified was in fact the person who was claiming to be the king of the Jews. Thus it is likely that the other Jesus (The Criminal), and not Jesus of Nazareth (Barabbas) or the Messiah, who was in fact crucified.

The Justice and Mercy of God

Christian theologians object to the Islamic theological belief that we need both Faith and Good Works together to be saved. The Qur'an states:

> **But those who believe and do righteous deeds - We will" admit them to gardens beneath which rivers flow..." (4:57)**

Protestant Christians believe In "justification by faith alone", while Catholics place a little more emphasis on actions. Yet all Christians would not claim that a person who believes in Jesus is free to commit sins and crimes and yet still expect to go to heaven. So at the end of the day, they also acknowledge that both faith and good works are needed.

The other objection they have is this: how can a sin committed against God be expiated by the repentance of a human? They claim that a sin against God can only be expiated by the action of God. The simple answer is that it God's will that faith and certain acts of repentance cancel out certain sins committed against God. Just as Christians claim (without basis) that Jesus' death was willed by God to a vehicle for salvation, why can it not be God's will that certain good works atone for certain sins? Surely, this is more just than believing that the sacrifice and pain of one person wipes away the sins of other, independent people.

ALLAH SENT US IMAMS TO GUIDE US AND CONTINUE THE MESSAGE OF THE PROPHETS

Section 6: Imamah

6.1- Imāmah

THE MEANING OF IMAMAH

As we discussed in previous lessons, Imāmah literally means leadership. However, we use it to specifically refer to divinely appointed leaders: people who were appointed to lead the Muslim community by God.

As Shīʿah, we believe that the position of leadership of the Muslim community is one of the most important issues in Islam. Without the most qualified leader, the Muslim community would stray from the right path and Islam itself would be compromised. When the Prophet (s) was alive, he was obviously the leader of the Muslim community. However, after his death, there was much dispute and controversy about this position.

Just as we need Prophets to show us the path to Allah (swt) and act as practical role models, we need Imams to guide us in the same way. Once the final Prophet's mission ended, there was a need for an Imam to perform some of the functions that a Prophet did, in order to protect the message and the mission. This leader, like the Prophets, must be divinely chosen and appointed, as if it were left to anyone else to choose this leader, then the wrong leader may be chosen (as in fact happened in history), and this would slowly lead the Muslim community in the wrong direction. Choosing a leader through consensus, voting or the opinion of one individual or a group of elite individuals leaves room for error and does not ensure that the correct and most qualified person is appointed as the leader.

[1] References for these narrations can be found in the books recommended below, as well as:

- Bukhārī, Vol. 8, Ḥadīth #127
- Muslim, Vol. 3, Ḥadīth #1452
- Refer to eHAWZA, semester 2, course 6, lecture 2 for more details

Unlike other Muslims, we believe that Allah (swt) and His Messenger would not leave the Muslim community without a leader who was chosen and appointed by Allah (swt). In fact, we believe that Allah (swt) instructed His Prophet (s) to appoint twelve successors, each of whom in turn would lead the Muslim community. It is impossible that the Prophet (s), who instructed the Muslims on the smallest of issues (such as which side to sleep on and which foot to walk out of the bathroom with) would not instruct them on who should be the leader (the Imām) after himself.

There is a significant amount of documented historical evidence for this from all Muslim sects, alongside evidence from the Qur'ān itself and logical reasoning as seen above [1].

Twelve Imāms

The Prophet (s) appointed twelve Imāms after himself. The first of these was Imām ʿAlī (ʿa). The last of these Imāms is Imām al-Mahdī (ʿaj), who is still alive today. He was born over 1200 years ago, and lives in occultation. We will have further discussions on Imām Mahdī (ʿaj) in future lessons.

> The Prophet (ṣ): "There will be twelve 'Amīrs...all of them from Quraysh." [2]

The Imāms are Divinely Protected from Sin (maʿṣūm)

One of our major beliefs is that the Imāms, just like the prophets, were sinless and immaculate (maʿṣūm). We have discussed in previous lessons that the Prophets were sinless and why they must be sinless. We also refuted objections against this belief.

[1] For further reference, please see the following works that are useful for learning factual information about our belief in Imāmah and the differences between the Shīʿah belief and the belief of other sects:

- Then I was Guided - Sayed Tijani Simawi- available online at al-islam.org
- Al-Murajʿāt - Sayyed Sharaful Dīn al-Musawī- available online at al-islam.org
- Al-Nas,wal-Ijtihād - Sayyed Sharaful Dīn al-Musawī, available online at al-islam.org:
- https://www.al-islam.org/al-nass-wal-ijtihad-text-and-interpretation-abd-al-husayn-sharaf-al-din-al-musawi
- Peshawar Nights - available online at al-islam.org

[2] Ṣaḥīḥ,Bukhārī, Vol.9, P. 279, Ḥadīth #. 2034

To quickly recap:

- We need a role model to follow, and the Imāms are our greatest role models along with the Prophets (ʿa). If they were not sinless we would have no point of reference to check our actions against.
- Secondly, if they were not sinless, we would not be sure that what they are telling us is in fact the command of Allah (swt) or otherwise, as they could be lying. This would undermine the very foundations of our faith.

The Imāms choose not to sin because of the special divine protection that God has blessed them with. This divine protection was blessed upon them because Allah (swt) knew in His infinite knowledge that they would have earned it eventually. Allah (swt) states in the Qur'ān that He chooses specific people for the position of being an Imām, that He inspires these Imāms to do good actions, and that the guidance they provide to people is always inspired by Allah (swt):

وَجَعَلْنَاهُمْ أَئِمَّةً يَهْدُونَ بِأَمْرِنَا وَأَوْحَيْنَا إِلَيْهِمْ فِعْلَ الْخَيْرَاتِ وَإِقَامَ الصَّلَاةِ وَإِيتَاءَ الزَّكَاةِ وَكَانُوا لَنَا عَابِدِينَ

"And We made them Imāms, guiding (mankind) by Our Command, and We inspired in them the doing of good deeds..." {21:73}

The Characteristics of the Imāms

In addition to being maʿṣūm, the Imām of the Muslim community must have the following characteristics.

1-The highest level of faith: For example, it is unanimously agreed that Imām ʿAlī (ʿa) never prostrated before any idol [1] whereas Abū Bakr, ʿUmar and ʿUthmān indisputably all worshipped idols at some time in their lives. Eight years had passed since the rise of Islam and ʿUmar (the second Caliph) was still an idolater! Even after embracing Islam, he would question the Prophet's decisions and cast doubt on them on various occasions. One example of this can be seen in the events surrounding the treaty of Ḥudaybiyyah. The Prophet (s) had a dream that the Muslims would perform Ḥajj and so they all set out towards Mecca. Before they reached there, the Quraysh confronted them in an aggressive manner and the Prophet (s) decided to enter into a treaty with them rather than engage in war. So the Muslims stopped their journey to Mecca and the Prophet asked them to shave their heads and to slaughter their animals of sacrifice, for they were not going to Ḥajj that year. ʿUmar was very upset by this and would not stop objecting to the Prophet's decision and even personally confronted the Prophet (s). However, the Prophet (s) told him that he had promised they would go to Ḥajj, but not that year [2].

2-The highest level of knowledge: This is also necessary for the leader of the Muslim community. In the āyah,

"Say: Are those who know equal to those who know not?" {39:9}

Allah clearly states that one of the traits that gives merit to an individual is when they possess true knowledge, which is knowledge about Allah.

The Prophet (s) said about Imām ʿAlī (ʿa):

"I am the city of knowledge, and 'Aīi is its gate. Whoever wishes to enter the city should enter it from its gate." [3]

[1] Al-Kashhāf, Vol. 4, P. 12; Tafsir al-Qurtubi, Vol. 15, P. 20; Rūh al-Maʿānī, Vol. 22, P. 225; Tafsīr al-Thaʿlabī, Vol. 8, P. 126

[2] Al-Nas,wal Ijtihād, p.198-202.

[3] Duʿā al-Nudbāʾ, Mafatīh,al-Jinān

In contrast to this, for example, ʿUmar would often be corrected in his Islamic knowledge. Examples include the time a woman stood up in the mosque one day to correct ʿUmar's ruling on dowries and a time when Imām ʿAlī (ʿa) stopped a woman from being wrongly executed due to ʿUmar's mistake.

One day, ʿUmar had become upset about the rising dowries within the Muslim community and so he ordered that there should be an upper limit on dowries. A woman stood up in the crowd and quoted the āyah: "...and if you had given her a heap of gold", which clearly showed that it was permissible to give a woman a very large dowry. Thus, ʿUmar was mistaken in his ruling and he admitted to this [1].

One day, Imām ʿAlī (ʿa) saw a mentally ill woman being prepared for execution. He inquired why this was happening and they said that she had committed adultery and was being punished. He stopped all the proceedings and brought the woman back before ʿUmar. He reminded ʿUmar of the narration which says that the pen (i.e. responsibility) is lifted from upon those who are mentally ill (among others) and so she could not be punished. Again, ʿUmar admitted his mistake and confessed that if it were not for the advice of Imām ʿAlī (ʿa), he would have perished [2].

3-The best in jihād: This is another necessity of leadership mentioned in the Qurʾān:

"Allah has preferred in grades those who strive hard and fight with their wealth and their lives above those who sit." {4:95}

There is no doubt that no one came close to Imām ʿAlī (ʿa) and his progeny in this category. The examples of the Battles of Khaybar and Uhud are two of the most famous.

4. Karāmāt: All our Imāms performed miracles of one form or another. Miracles performed by the Imāms are called karāmāt.

[1] Al-Sunan al-Kubrā, Vol. 7, P. 233; Kanz al-ʿUmmāl, Vol. 8, P. 298

[2] Sunan Abī Dāwūd, Vol. 2, P. 227; Sunan Ibn Mājeh, Vol. 2, P. 227; Al-Mustadrak ʿala al-Sahihayn, Vol. 2, P. 59; Sahih al-Bukhārī, Vol. 6, P. 2499

5. Exalted character: All our Imāms (ʿa) have the highest level of etiquette and manners which they learnt directly from the Noble Prophet (s). They practiced and taught Makārim al-Akhlāq (the noblest of moral traits).

6. Justice: The Imāms all practiced and taught the highest forms of justice. Unfortunately, because of these very characteristics, all our Imāms (ʿa) were mistreated by a certain segment of the population. Many were imprisoned for extended periods of time and all of the first 11 Imāms were eventually killed. The people around them had immense jealousy, hatred, and malice toward them, and feared that their power would be challenged by the Imāms and their followers. The major enemies of the Imāms were always hypocrites: people who pretended to be Muslims and to care about Islam but who had only personal interests in mind.

The Imāms are not Chosen by People

It is important to understand that Imāms are not chosen by people through election. Rather, they are chosen by Allah (swt) because they possess the above characteristics. It is only Allah (swt) who can make this appointment and give this position to someone. According to the Noble Qurʾān, even Prophets do not appoint their successors. When Prophet Mūsā (ʿa) wanted a successor to help him in his mission, he asked Allah (swt) to appoint this successor, rather than appointing one himself {20:29-36}. Similarly, when Prophet Ibrāhīm (ʿā) was appointed as an Imām, he did not choose his successor. Instead, he asked Allah (swt) to choose successors from his offspring {2:124}.

Throughout history, when people have been appointed or chosen through an election, they made major mistakes that have led to disastrous consequences for the Muslim community. We also see how many so-called 'world leaders' today, who are at least at a superficial level elected by people, make decisions that end up harming the majority of human beings.

The Status of the Ahl al-Bayt (ʿa)

Part of our belief in Imāmah is our belief about the Ahl al-Bayt and their great status. ‘Ahl al-Bayt’ literally means ‘people of the household’, but it is a specific Qur’ānic term referring to certain members of the household of the Prophet (s). These people are:

- The Prophet (s) himself
- Imām ‘Ali (ʿa)- his cousin and son-in-law
- Sayyidah Fāṭimah (ʿa)- his daughter
- Imām Ḥasan (ʿa) and
- Imām Ḥusayn (ʿa)- his grandsons.

In the Noble Qur’ān, Allah (swt) says the following about the Ahl al-Bayt:

إِنَّمَا يُرِيدُ اللَّهُ لِيُذْهِبَ عَنكُمُ الرِّجْسَ أَهْلَ الْبَيْتِ وَيُطَهِّرَكُمْ تَطْهِيرًا

"Allah only desires to keep away impurity from you, Oh People of the House (Ahl al-Bayt) and to purify you with a (thorough) purification." {33:33}

The above āyah, by clearly stating that Allah has removed all impurity from the Ahl al-Bayt, confirms that they are sinless and protected from any impurity due to Divine protection [1]. This is the sinlessness (‘ismah) that we have discussed earlier.

There is some discussion about who this āyah applies to. However, numerous narrations, found in both Shīʿah and Sunni books of narration, indicate clearly that the āyah refers to the five people listed above [2].

Now that we know that the Noble Qur’ān confirms that the Ahl al-Bayt are sinless, immaculate, and have a special divine protection and great status in the eyes of Allah (swt), let us look at what type of relationship we should have with the Ahl al-Bayt.

[1] Tafsīr al-Mīzān, discussion of āyah 33:33

[2] Other schools of thought indicate that it may be referring to the wives of the Prophet (s) because the above expression comes in the context of āyāt which are speaking about the wives of the Prophet. However, this opinion is clearly incorrect for the following reasons: The āyah uses the expression ‘ankum’, which in Arabic refers either to the masculine or a group including male members. Therefore it cannot refer to the wives of the Prophet. If it was referring to them, the expression used would have to be ‘ankunna’. There are a great number of narrations that indicate that this āyah was revealed about the five people mentioned above. These narrations are narrated through both Sunnī and Shīʿah chains of narration. In fact, the Sunnī chains of narration are greater in number, and they amount to more than forty; Al-Kāfī, Vol. 1, P. 187

The above āyah, by clearly stating that Allah has removed all impurity from the Ahl al-Bayt, confirms that they are sinless and protected from any impurity due to Divine protection. This is the sinlessness ('ismah) that we have discussed earlier.

There is some discussion about who this āyah applies to. However, numerous narrations, found in both Shīʿah and Sunni books of narration, indicate clearly that the āyah refers to the five people listed above.

Now that we know that the Noble Qur'ān confirms that the Ahl al-Bayt are sinless, immaculate, and have a special divine protection and great status in the eyes of Allah (swt), let us look at what type of relationship we should have with the Ahl al-Bayt.

Our Relationship with the Ahl al-Bayt (ʻa)

As we discussed, the Ahl al-Bayt are sinless. Therefore, they are the examples that we should follow in all aspects of our life, if we want to save ourselves from straying from the right path. In fact, the Noble Prophet (s) says: (this is narrated from multiple Sunni and Shīʿah chains of narration)

"The likeness of my Ahl al-Bayt amongst my Ummah (followers) is similar to Noah's Ark. Those who embark on it are rescued and those who reject it are perished...." [1]

[1] Al-Hakīm, Al-Mustadrak, 3:163; al-Sayuti, Ihya al Mayyit, p. 248

Not only are we urged to follow the Ahl al-Bayt and to hold on to them as role models and guides, but we are also expected to build the love for the Ahl al-Bayt in ourselves and our families. Love for the Ahl al-Bayt is not only a form of worship, but the highest one.

Imām Ṣādiq (ʿa) says: "Surely, there are various degrees of serving Allah, but affection for us, the Ahl al-Bayt, is the highest one." [1]

This is because if we love the Ahl al-Bayt then we will naturally incline towards following their example, and since they are the most perfect of people who are closest to Allah (swt), we will naturally incline towards being perfect servants of Allah (swt).

[1] Biḥar al-Anwār, Vol. 27, P. 91

Love for the Ahl al-Bayt manifests itself in a number of ways:

- Taking them as role models
- Learning the knowledge they passed on to us
- Obeying them in all matters
- Loving those who love them and disassociating ourselves from the actions and lifestyle of those who show enmity towards them

Ḥadīth al-Thaqalayn

Prophet Muhammad (s) has promised two weighty things which will never separate from each other and will provide guidance if we attach ourselves to them. The two things have been mentioned in the acclaimed narration known as Ḥadīth al-Thaqalayn. This ḥadīth, or narration, has been narrated from several different narrators and has been granted the status mutawātir, meaning there is no doubt about its authenticity in any of the schools of thought. Additionally, it is not only accepted by the different schools of thought, but has been mentioned in the ḥadīth books of the different schools. The text varies slightly in each narration but the core message is the same.

This particular narration of Ḥadīth al-Thaqalayn is referenced in Al-Kāfī, which is one of the four most important Shīʿah sources of ḥadīth and is reported there as:

إِنِّي تَارِكٌ فِيكُمْ أَمْرَيْنِ إِنْ أَخَذْتُمْ بِهِمَا لَنْ تَضِلُّوا- كِتَابَ اللَّهِ عَزَّ وَ جَلَّ وَ أَهْلَ بَيْتِي عِتْرَتِي أَيُّهَا النَّاسُ اسْمَعُوا وَ قَدْ بَلَّغْتُ إِنَّكُمْ سَتَرِدُونَ عَلَيَّ الْحَوْضَ فَأَسْأَلُكُمْ عَمَّا فَعَلْتُمْ فِي الثَّقَلَيْنِ وَ الثَّقَلَانِ كِتَابُ اللَّهِ جَلَّ ذِكْرُهُ وَ أَهْلُ بَيْتِي

"Truly I am leaving two things among you, to which if you hold yourself, you will never go astray: the book of Allah- Invincible and Majestic is He and my Ahl al-Bayt (ʿa), my ʿitrah (family). O people! Listen! And I have delivered the message to you: definitely, you will enter my presence at the pond, and I will ask you about what you did to the two weighty things, and the Thaqalayn is the Book of Allah - exalted is His mention and my Ahl al-Bayt (ʿa)."

Sunan an-Nasāʾī , one of the six Ṣaḥīḥ books of the Sunnis, quotes it in this way:

كَأَنِّي قَدْ دُعِيتُ فَأَجَبْتُ، إِنِّي قَدْ تَرَكْتُ فِيكُمُ الثَّقَلَيْنِ: أَحَدُهُمَا أَكْبَرُ مِنَ الآخَرِ، كِتَابُ اللَّهِ تَعَالَى، وَعِتْرَتِي، فَانْظُرُوا كَيْفَ تَخْلُفُونِي فِيهِمَا، فَإِنَّهُمَا لَنْ يَتَفَرَّقَا حَتَّى يَرِدَا عَلَيَّ الْحَوْضَ "

"It is as if I have been called, and so I have answered. Truly I have left the Thaqalayn (two weighty things) among you, one of them is greater from the other, the book of Allah and my ʿitrah (Ahl al-Bayt (ʿa)). So look after how you will behave with them after me, indeed they will never separate from each other until they enter my presence by the pool.

Not only are we urged to follow the Ahl al-Bayt and to hold on to them as role models and guides, but we are also expected to build the love for the Ahl al-Bayt in ourselves and our families. Love for the Ahl al-Bayt is not only a form of worship, but the highest one.

It is an undeniable ḥadīth, and even contemporary Salafī scholars, like Muḥammad Nāṣir al-Dīn Al-Bānī, accept it. The other versions of Kitāb and Sunnah are weak.

The tradition denotes three major ideological points:

- obligation to follow the Noble Qurʾān and Ahl al-Bayt (ʿa);
- infallibility of Ahl al-Bayt (ʿa) because they are inseparable from the Noble Qurʾān;
- continuation of Imāmah since the two will be the source of guidance until the Day of Judgment.

The Noble Prophet (s) announced the intertwined nature of these two - he wanted to establish for mankind that guidance is provided only by the Divine in the form of the Imāms and the Noble Qurʾān until the Day of Judgment. Practically speaking, we should be looking to the Noble Qurʾān and traditions of the Ahl al-Bayt (ʿa) for all of our intellectual, practical, and jurisprudential needs.

The Importance of Imamah

The concept of 'Imāmah' or Divine Leadership is so significant in Islam that Allah (swt) says that on the Day of Judgement, He will call on every nation by their Imām or leader (i.e. the one they accepted as their leader) {17:71}. Allah (swt) gives the people of Pharaoh as an example. They accepted the misguided leadership of Pharaoh and because of this the Qur'ān states on the Judgment Day they will be forced to follow Pharaoh into the Hellfire {40:46}.

We see that people today and throughout history have agreed to be led by evil doers and tyrants such as Pharaoh, or Mu'āwiyah. The Qur'ān teaches us that this will have the most dire consequences for these people in the Hereafter. In contrast, we who identify ourselves as Shī'ah Muslims choose the very best of God's creation–the Ahl al-Bayt ('a)–as our leaders and we follow their path. We hope that this means that on Judgment Day they will lead us along with them into Paradise.

6.2-Imām ʿAlī (ʿa)

THE FIRST IMAM

We have learnt that Allah (swt) appointed 12 divine guides- Imams- to lead the Muslim community after the death of the Prophet (saw). Th first of these Imams was Imām ʿAlī (ʿa)- the Prophet's cousin, son-in-law and closest friend and companion.

Perhaps one of the most difficult times in the life of Imām ʿAlī (ʿa) happened 11 years after Hijrah on the 28th of Ṣafar. It was on this day that this world lost the best of humans–the Noble Prophet Muḥammad (s), and Imām ʿAlī (ʿa) lost his brother. He was one of the only people with maʿrifah–true understanding– of the nūr of the Prophet (s), and this which made losing the Prophet (s) very difficult.

During this time, many people wanted to prevent Imām ʿAlī (ʿa) from being the successor of Prophet Muḥammad (s) because they wanted power for themselves. They saw an opportunity to steer people away from the Imāms and acted as if the Noble Prophet (s) was not in his senses when he passed away.

Calamity of Thursday

Three days before his death, the Prophet (s) lay on his deathbed, knowing the end was near. With his companions by his side, he requested a pen and said, "Now let me write something for you, with it you shall not go astray after me." He wanted to leave behind his will and name his successor one final time.

ʿUmar ibn Khaṭṭāb said, "The Prophet is overcome by illness; we have the Qurʾān, the Book of Allah (swt), which is sufficient for us." So, people did not let the Prophet (s) write his will down. It was partly because of this event, the Calamity of Thursday, that there was so much confusion after his passing.

On the fateful day of his death, his wife Umm Salamah narrated, "By Allah, the closest person [to the Prophet] at the time of his death was ʿAlī (ʿa). Early in the morning of the day when he was going to die, the Prophet (s) called ʿAlī (ʿa) who had been sent out on some errand. He asked for ʿAlī (ʿa) three times before his return. However, ʿAlī (ʿa) came before sunrise. So, thinking that the Prophet (s) needed some privacy with ʿAlī (ʿa), we came out. I was the last to be out; therefore, I sat closer to the door than the other women. I saw that ʿAlī (ʿa) lowered his head towards the Prophet (s) and the Prophet (s) kept whispering into his ears (for sometime). ʿAlī (ʿa) was the only person who was [sitting] with the Prophet (s) till the end."

After much dispute and having ignored the declaration of Rasūlullāh (s) at Ghadīr Khumm that Imām ʿAlī (ʿa) was his successor, the people chose Abū Bakr as their Caliph. Everyone was asked to pledge allegiance to him. Imām ʿAlī (ʿa) refused to do so because it was his right and duty to lead the Muslims.

ʿUmar tried to force Imām ʿAīi (ʿa) to pledge allegiance, even burning the door of his house. Many other atrocities were committed against the Ahl al-Bayt within a matter of days such as, a rope being tied around Imām Ali (ʿa) 's neck to force him to come to the masjid to pledge allegiance to Abū Bak. The estate of Fadak, which that Rasūlullāh (s) had given to his daughter Sayyidah Fātịmah (ʿa) was also being taken away by force from her.

Overnight, the Ahl al-Bayt (ʿa) of Rasūlullāh (s) were isolated, alone, and oppressed. For the short period that she lived after Rasūlullāh (s), Sayyidah Fāṭimah (ʿa) cried day and night and called out to her father, "Such afflictions have befallen me (after you), If they were to befall on a day, it would change to a dark night!"

The first calamity happened even before the Prophet (s) was buried. As Imām ʿAlī (ʿa) washbathed the body of the Noble Prophet (s) and performed the funeral rites, some of the Ansạr and Muhajirūn gathered at a place called Saqīfah Banī Saʿīdah. With ill intentions , filled with greed for power, they began discussing the leadership of the Muslims, now that the Prophet (s) was gone. They came up with many excuses as to why Imām ʿAlī (ʿa) could not be the leader of the Muslims. Some said he was too young, and others claimed that Abū Bakr was the first person to accept Islam. In the end, they chose Abū Bakr to be the first khalīfah.

We know that at Ghadīr Khumm, Prophet Muḥammad (s) gathered the Muslims to remind them that Imām ʿAlī (ʿa) was his successor. He gave a full sermon and proclaimed "Whoever I am the master of, ʿAlī is his master." This account is in both Shīʿah and Sunnī sources, but some try to explain the meaning of "mawlā" or "master" to "friend", or they have taken out this phrase. We know that the Prophet (s) declared Imām ʿAlī (ʿa) to be his successor on many other occasions, and demonstrated to others that Imām ʿAlī (ʿa) had a unique status that was bestowed upon him by Allah (swt). station in battles and in the eyes of Allah.

Imām ʿAlī (ʿa) tried to remind the people of the Prophet's (s) declaration at Ghadīr and other places, but it was useless. Abū Bakr and his supporter ʿUmar threatened those who opposed them. Imām ʿAlī (ʿa) did not want to cause fitnah (disunity) amongst the Muslim ummah, so he remained silent, saying, "The religion of Islam is too great for me to cause disunity. I will remain silent, but when I see injustice, I will speak out against it." Imām ʿAlī (ʿa) had the wisdom to know that this was the best course of action during this time. The circumstances dictated it best for him to remain silent.

So, Imām ʿAlī (ʿa) remained silent and patient during these long, difficult 25 years. First, he watched as his beloved wife and the daughter of Rasūlullāh (s), Sayyidah Fāṭimah az-Zahrāʾ (ʿa), was troubled at the hands of the new khilāfah. The garden of Fadak, which the Prophet (s) gifted to her, was wrongfully taken away from her by Abū Bakr. She went to the masjid to give a powerful sermon about this from behind a curtain, but her focus was not on the material loss. She gave this sermon to remind people of their love for the Prophet (s) and that Imām ʿAlī (ʿa) was his rightful successor, appointed by Allah (swt).

But the tragedy reached its peak when the khalīfah sent men to Imām ʿAlī's (ʿa) door to demand his allegiance. Sayyidah Fāṭimah (ʿa), who was pregnant with her son Muḥsin, went to the door to turn them away. The oppressors burned and knocked down the door, crushing her between the door and the wall, killing Muḥsin. Soon after, she passed away from the injuries she sustained from this tragic event. Once more, Imām ʿAlī (ʿa) had to bury someone so dear and precious to him. Sayyidah Fāṭimah (ʿa) asked Imām ʿAlī (ʿa) to bury her in secret because of the injustices and oppression she suffered from the Ummah.

Now, left all alone, Imām ʿAlī (ʿa) had no choice but to guide the people by any means possible. This was difficult, since the khalīfah had turned many people against him. During these years, aside from the few true companions he had left, people would not even say salām to Amīr ul-Muʿminīn. They had rejected him to the point where they would not let him work for them and he had to work in the orchard of a Jewish person for three years.

During these 25 years of silence, Imām ʿAlī (ʿa) used his time planning for the future of the ummah. He began developing and planning the infrastructure for an Islamic government. He also took this opportunity to compile the Noble Qurʾān that we have today and guide others in any way he could.

Additionally, whenever a problem came up for the khalīfahs that they did not know how to solve, they would turn to Imām ʿAlī (ʿa). Imām ʿAlī (ʿa) never turned them away, and would help them solve their problems because he knew it would help the Muslims.

Abū Bakr once said, "May Allah never put me in a situation where I do not have access to Abūl Ḥasan to solve a problem."

Abū Bakr was only khalīfah for three years before he died. After him, the position was taken by ʿUmar. During his khilāfah, ʿUmar said 70 times, "If ʿAlī (ʿa) had not been there, ʿUmar would have perished." Once again, this shows how they understood the rightful position and status of Imām ʿAlī (ʿa).

After ʿUmar passed away, the khilāfah was given to ʿUthmān, who had bad advisors, and thus did not have good strategies or sound political judgment. For example, he appointed his family members to government positions, although they were corrupt and unqualified. Specifically, he allowed his cousin Mu'awiyah to remain as governor of Sham (modern-day Syria) and to build a major power base there. Slowly, the people's anger towards this corruption rose, until finally, it led to the assassination of ʿUthmān by a group of people that had become frustrated with his governance.

Imām ʿAlī (ʿa) , who was once the most active individual in service of Islam, now stayed at home. For the next 25 years, he simply 'disappeared' from the public. He remained oppressed and was denied his right continuously.

The Prophet's (s) passing was only the beginning of difficulties for the Ahl al-Bayt (ʿa). Imām ʿAlī (ʿa) describes these 25 years from the Prophet's (s) riḥlah to his khilāfah as a period of patience. He said, "I adopted patience although there was pricking in the eye and suffocation in the throat. I watched the plundering of my inheritance till the first one went his way, but handed over the khilāfah to [ʿUmar] Ibn al-Khaṭṭāb after himself."

This saying can be found in Nahj al-Balāghah, a compilation of sermons and letters of Imām ʿAlī (ʿa). In this sermon, Imām ʿAlī (ʿa) explains to the Muslims what happened after the riḥlah of Rasūlullāh (s). For the Imāms—who have maʿrifah of Allah—it is very difficult to see people suffer because they are infallible, and they know what is best for people.

After that, the people went and pleaded to Imām ʿAlī (ʿa) to become the next khalīfah, but he did not accept right away. He knew that after so many years of corruption, it would be hard to rule justly and Islamically. Thus, he wanted to make sure people knew what they were asking for.

There were so many people who had come to beg Imām ʿAlī (ʿa) to take the position that Imām Ḥasan (ʿa) and Imām Ḥusayn (ʿa) were scared that they would be trampled. Imām ʿAlī (ʿa) described the event as saying, "They came in like thirsty camels that had finally found their water."

Finally, after continuous insistence from the people, Imām ʿAlī (ʿa) accepted the position. However, he made it very clear that he was only taking the khilāfah as a responsibility upon him and not out of his own desire. He said in one of his sermons that, "The world in front of me is less valuable than the snot of a goat." He did not want the khilāfah for the sake of greed or a thirst for power like those who tried to take it from him. He knew that people needed to be guided Islamically, politically, and socially, by a just leader.

Therefore, he started a government with justice, but because people had fallen for material gains and striving for this world in favour ofversus the hereafter, he spent much of his time as khalīfah in war. This was the beginning of the outward animosity towards our Imāms, and every Imām until the 11th Imām (ʿa) was martyred because of this same reason.

6.3

LADY FĀṬIMAH (ʿA)

Sayyidah Fāṭimah (ʿa) is the daughter of Prophet Muḥammad (s). She has been given many special honours by Allah (swt), including being described as the leader of the women of the worlds. She was the only child of Prophet Muḥammad (s) through whom he had grandchildren and lineage.

Lady Fāṭimah had three roles that she fulfilled perfectly: family life, being a mujāhidah (one who struggles in the path of Allah), and being an ʿābidah (one who worships Allah). We will discuss the next part of her life, her family life up to the passing of Prophet Muḥammad (s), in light of these three roles.

Marriage to Imām ʿAlī (ʿa) to Prophet's Riḥlah

Due to widespread conditions of near poverty of many Muslims during the early years after the migration, Sayyidah Fāṭimah (ʿa) would spend her day working on household chores, while upbringing her children and praying for many hours a day. She worked to the point where blisters formed on her hands, a scar formed on her chest from carrying heavy water holders, and she was in a lot of pain.

Imām ʿAlī (ʿa) said to her, "Why don't you ask your father? He might know a servant to help around the house."

Lady Fāṭimah (ʿa) went to the Prophet's house, but was too shy to ask him, since he had some guests present, so she returned home.

The next day, the Prophet (s) visited them, and, from Allah (swt), he had the knowledge of what she had wanted to ask.

The Noble Prophet (s) told Lady Fāṭimah (ʿa), "Shall I teach you something that is better for you than a servant and a world with everything in it? After every prayer say: Allāhu Akbar thirty four times, then Alhạmdulillāh thirty three times and Subhạ̄nallāh thirty three times. Surely this is better for you than that which you wanted,the world, and its belongings.'

This tasbīh. of Sayyidah Fāṭimah (ʿa) is a blessing and tool for us in instances of hardship, and is recommended to be recited after every prayer. After a few years, the Noble Prophet (s) gifted her a servant named Fiḍḍạ̄. However, Lady Fiḍḍạ̄ would work one day, and then Lady Fāṭimah (ʿa) the next. In this way, there was justice, and the servant was not overworked nor did she feel humiliated.

Tarbiyah of her Children

Sayyidah Fāṭimah (ʿa) and Imām ʿAlī (ʿa) had four living children together, and Sayyidah Fāṭimah took care to raise them in the best way. She taught them the best of manners and encouraged them to learn from and spend time with their father and grandfather.

It seems that Imām Ḥasan had made it a habit to wake up in the early hours of the night and join his mother, Sayyidah Fāṭimah az-Zahrāʾ (ʿa) in her tahạjjud (night prayers). Imām Ḥasan (ʿa) observed that his mother prayed for believing men and women. When the prayers were over, he said, "Mother, you prayed for everyone, but I did not hear a word for yourself or anyone in the family!" Sayyidah Fāṭimah az-Zahrāʾ (ʿa) replied, "O my son Ḥasan, remember one thing neighbors come first and then one's household follows."

With her own actions, paired with wise words, she was able to impart valuable lessons to all of her children.

Lady Fāṭimah (ʿa), in her care towards her family, starting from her father to her entire family up until the time of her death, taught us the importance of family. She used to answer questions about Islam from other women at the time, and at times of need she assisted her father in his mission. But most of her efforts took place inside the private sphere of the home and not in the public eye. She showed us that success is not always found in being public and taking on visible roles.

We can see from Sayyidah Fāṭimah (ʿa) that engaging in self-praise or self-idolizing is not constructive in being successful. A common form of self-idolizing is social media. The primary purpose of many social media platforms has become self-idolizing and showing off to others. Self-praise, in many cases, can be detrimental to spiritual growth and gaining nearness to Allah (swt), despite how normal it has become in some cultures.

Sayyidah Fāṭimah (ʿa) was so successful despite never fighting in a battle, formally teaching in a university, or writing a book. She did dictate to Imām ʿAlī the predictions the angels gave her and that has been compiled into a book we know as Mushạf Fāṭimah. Lady Fāṭimah was so successful and beloved to Allah, through being the best worshipper and fulfilling all of her duties.

The Event of Mubāhalah

In the 8th year after Hijrah, the Prophet (s) was challenged to a debate by the Christians of Najran regarding the status of Prophet ʿĪsā (ʿa). After this group stubbornly refused to accept his logical arguments, Allah (swt) commanded the Prophet (s) to challenge them to a mubāhalah. A mubāhalah is a type of spiritual battle between two groups where they both pray to Allah to remove His mercy from the group that is incorrect and misguided. This clarifies who is correct when there is disagreement.

Allah said to Rasūlullāh (s):

فَمَنْ حَآجَّكَ فِيهِ مِنۢ بَعْدِ مَا جَآءَكَ مِنَ ٱلْعِلْمِ فَقُلْ تَعَالَوْا۟ نَدْعُ أَبْنَآءَنَا وَأَبْنَآءَكُمْ وَنِسَآءَنَا وَنِسَآءَكُمْ وَأَنفُسَنَا وَأَنفُسَكُمْ ثُمَّ نَبْتَهِلْ فَنَجْعَل لَّعْنَتَ ٱللَّهِ عَلَى ٱلْكَـٰذِبِينَ

"Should anyone argue with you concerning him, after the knowledge that has come to you, say, 'Come! Let us call our sons and your sons, our women and your women, our souls and your souls, then let us pray earnestly, and call down Allah's curse upon the liars." {3:61}

The next day, the Prophet (s) went for the mubāhalah and took with him four individuals: his sons [Imām Ḥasan (ʿa) and Imām Ḥusayn (ʿa)], his women [Sayyidah Fāṭimah (ʿa)], and the one who was so close to him it's as if he was his own self [Imām ʿAlī (ʿa)]. When the Christians saw the faithful faces of the Ahl al-Bayt (ʿa) radiating with nūr (light), they realized they were misguided and immediately backed away from the challenge.

In spite of the fact that 'our women' is a plural noun in Arabic and includes at least three people, the Noble Prophet (s) took only Lady Fāṭimah (ʿa). This shows that she fulfilled the meaning of all of the women in that verse and that there was no woman like her. Conversely, the Christians had brought many women to represent them. The Prophet (s) chose the Ahl al-Bayt, only five people including himself, to represent all of Islam at the Event of Mubāhala because of their high spiritual status and their truthfulness. This indicates the purity (ṭahārah) of these individuals from sin as well!

The Bishop of Najrān, who had come to face the Ahl al-Bayt (ʿa), said of the five personalities, "I see faces such that if someone asked Allah through them to move a mountain from its place, he would move the mountain."

Ḥadīth al-Kisāʾ

In Ḥadīth al-Kisāʾ, we learn about the status of the Ahl al-Bayt (ʿa). In the Qurʾān, Allah revealed Āyah Taṭhīr, which was revealed on the event of the cloak—al-Kisāʾ:

إِنَّمَا يُرِيدُ ٱللَّهُ لِيُذْهِبَ عَنكُمُ ٱلرِّجْسَ أَهْلَ ٱلْبَيْتِ وَيُطَهِّرَكُمْ تَطْهِيرًا

"Indeed, Allah desires to keep away all impurity from you, O People of the Household, and purify you with a thorough purification." {33:33}

In this event, the Noble Prophet (s) was not feeling well, and he visited the house of his daughter, Sayyidah Fāṭimah (ʿa) and asked for a Yemeni cloak.

One by one, the members of the Ahl al-Bayt (ʿa) came to the door of Sayyidah Fāṭimah's house and asked for her permission to enter her home. Her sons, Imām Ḥasan and Imām Ḥusayn (ʿa), came one after the other, and addressed her by saying, "Peace be upon you, O mother." She replied to each of them, "And upon you be peace, O light of my eyes, and the delight of my heart."

Imām ʿAlī (ʿa) addressed her by saying, "Peace be on you, O daughter of the Prophet (s) of Allah", and she replied, "And upon you be peace, O father of Ḥasan, and the Commander of the Faithful."

They then entered the room and asked the Prophet (s) if they could join him under the cloak. Soon, the Prophet (s) was joined by Imām Ḥasan (ʿa), Imām Ḥusayn (ʿa), Imām ʿAlī (ʿa), and Sayyidah Fāṭimah (ʿa). At this point, Rasūlullāh (s) expressed to Allah that these are the people of his household—the Ahl al-Bayt. The ḥādīth says, Allah told Jibrāʾīl, this is Fāṭimah, her children, her husband, and her father. The description of these people was done through Lady Fāṭimah which indicates her very high status.

The Prophet (s) mentioned how special these four people are to him and prayed to Allah to bless them and remove from them all impurities. Allah then told his angels that He created this entire world and everything in it only for the love of these five individuals. He then sent Angel Jibraʾīl to join them under the cloak and inform the Prophet (s) that his duʿā had been accepted.

Lady Fāṭimah raised Imām Ḥasan (ʿa), Imām Ḥusayn (ʿa), Sayyidah Zaynab, and Sayyidah Umm Kulthūm as the best of role models. She dedicated her time to ensure the success of the believers through these blessed children.
When the Prophet (s) was close to leaving this world, he consoled Lady Fāṭimah and whispered something in her ear that gave her the strength to bear her dear father's death. It is said that he told her that she would soon join him in leaving this world.
In the 11th year after Hijrah, the Noble Prophet (s) passed away. With the death of Rasūlullāh came the hardest time for Ahl al-Bayt.

6.4 Imām Mahdī (ʿaj)

THE UNIVERSAL SAVIOR AND THE LIVING IMĀM

Imām al-Mahdī (ʿaj) is the 12th and final divinely appointed Imām from the progeny of Prophet Muhammad (s). He was born on 15 Shaʿbān, 255 AH and has been in hiding from that time until now. He is currently living on Earth, but is in hiding. He sees us and is aware of the events that occur in the world, but we do not recognize him or see his actions in the world.

He was born at the time of the Abbasid Caliph al-Muʿtamid, who had tried to prevent Imām Ḥasan al-ʿAskarī (ʿa) from having any children. However, the Imām was born undetected by the spies of the oppressive government. The true Shīʿahs were waiting for Imām al-ʿAskarī to announce his successor, and after the birth of Imām al-Mahdī (ʿaj), only a handful of true followers were told.

Allah (swt) granted the Imām (ʿa) with wisdom and excellence at birth. Like the Prophets ʿĪsā (ʿa) and Yahyā (ʿa), he had the ability to speak as an infant and would recite verses of the Noble Qurʾān from the cradle.

As we have seen from previous lessons, Imām al-Mahdī (ʿa) is the living Imām of our age. He has already been born and is living among us. The Ahl as-Sunnah believe that he is still to be born. We, however, believe that Imām al-Mahdī (ʿa) is alive but is hidden from us. We await his re-appearance, by the command of Allah (swt).

Some of the titles of the Imām (ʿaj) are:

- al-Qāʾim (the One who Rises)
- al-Ḥujjah (the Proof)
- al-Muntaḍar (the Awaited One)
- al-Muntaḍir (the Waiting One)
- Ṣaḥib uz-Zamān (Master of this Age)

Our Need for a Living Hujjah

At all times, this Earth needs a ḥujjah–a divine representative appointed by Allah (swt) – just as the shining sun is necessary for life on earth. Allah created this universe for us to reach perfection, which we learned in previous lessons can only be done through divine guides and revelation. Although Imām al-Mahdī is in occultation, he is still an active guide on the earth. An example that is used in the ḥadīth about our Imām in occultation is that he is like the sun behind the clouds. Although he is hidden from us, we still benefit from his light. We are not hidden from him. He has knowledge of the state of those who believe in him. .

Balancing Hope and Fear

The presence of the Imām is full of blessings, rooted in peace, tranquility, justice, and fairness. Because we are limited by our own knowledge, we can have a misunderstanding of what the Imām will actually do. When we think of the Imām returning, we sometimes think of this as being a fearful time. Since many people are going to be against him, we may fear that we are not going to be amongst his followers. We may also think of this as a time of destruction. Is it correct to have this type of fear?

Based on ḥadīths, the return of the Imām will bring justice to the oppressed. The Imam's miracles and the truth of his mission will be very clear. As he works to uproot oppression and tyranny from the Earth, more and more people will see the greatness of his mission, and will no longer be influenced by the tyrants. Many people will answer his call and join his mission. Only the arrogant leaders of oppression and the most stubborn of people will persist in fighting the Imām (ʿaj).

Islam is a religion that is balanced in every way, so we should be balanced between our fear of Allah and our belief in the mercy of Allah. For example, an excessive belief in mercy may lead us to think that Allah will forgive everything that we do, even if we are sinning intentionally. However, our repentance may not be sincere in this case. If we have too much fear of Allah, then we may become hopeless and stop striving to do better.

In the same way, we should have hope of the faraj of the Imām, while also being fearful of our own selves and our role within that reappearance. This should motivate us to be truly anticipating his arrival, which is the stage of doing Intiẓār.

The Importance of al-Intiẓār

> "The greatest worship of a believing ʿabd is waiting for the relief from Allah."

The narrations indicate that waiting for relief from Allah (swt) includes al-Intiẓār (actively waiting) for the reappearance of al-Mahdī (ʿaj). This is one of the greatest and most important and rewarding actions. His title al-Muntaẓar also indicates that people are waiting for him. In fact, there are ḥadīths from the Prophets and Imāms saying that they were waiting for the dhuhūr.

Waiting for the reappearance of the Imām, and truly living as one who is waiting, prepares a person to become a companion of the Imām at the time of his reappearance. Even if this person does not live long enough to witness the reappearance of the Imām, they will still gain the rewards of being counted as part of his companions. "The one who dies while anticipating the coming of the Imām (ʿaj), it is as if he was in the tent of the Imām. In fact, it is as if he was fighting the enemies alongside the Messenger of Allah (s)."

Al-Intiẓār (Waiting with Alertness)

This is the state we are supposed to be in while waiting for our Imām (ʿaj). It is not waiting lazily or passively. It is the active anticipation that involves preparation and eagerness for the Imām's arrival, and hope in a better future.

What We are Waiting For

Sometimes it becomes easy for us to believe that our society is currently good. We may become comfortable in our life. However, we are truly at loss without having the presence of our current Imām. Although we may have indirect guidance from him in different forms, such as the guidance of our ʿulamāʾ and the Imām's (ʿaj) presence even during occultation, having direct guidance from the Imām (ʿa) is among the best of blessings.

We can perhaps get a glimpse of what it will be like to receive direct guidance from the Imām (ʿa) from our past experiences. If you have ever been to ziyārah, at times, you may have felt the presence of the Imāms (ʿa) in their ḥarams. In Muḥarram, you may also feel the presence of the Imāms and experience a change inside of yourself and find yourself wanting to become even closer to the Imāms and further act on their teachings.

Some people may be ashamed of being in the presence of the Imām (ʿa) due to their past sins. But let us remember that just like we can always repent to Allah while we are alive, similarly, the gate towards prosperity through our Imāms' mercy and acceptance is always open regardless of how shameful one may be due to wrong decisions and actions.

We also see that there are many social problems and oppression around the world. Although we should make our best efforts to solve these problems, our efforts will not reach completion and perfection until after the return of the Imām (ʿaj). We should also remember that the return of the Imām (ʿaj) is the promise of Allah (swt), which we should not take lightly.

Dimensions of al-Intiẓār

1. Know the Imām: Find out as much as you can about your Imām (ʿaj), because the one who dies without knowing the Imām dies the death of ignorance and disbelief. More important than historical and biographical details is knowing what he stands for and what he wants from you.
2. Show your love for the Imām: Remembering him often, especially on happy occasions; giving charity on his behalf; and attending gatherings where he is mentioned.
3. Develop an emotional connection with the Imām (ʿa): Pray special supplications and prayers for the Imām (ʿa), write letters to him, and talk with him.
4. Act on your knowledge and love: Perform the deeds that you think the Imām would want you to do. Involve yourself in projects and programs that you think improve the community, and that the Imām (ʿa) would approve of.
5. Self growth or monitoring self: Constantly have the mindset of enhancing your own beliefs, ethics, and deeds (mushāraṭa, murāqabah, muḥāsabah).

Becoming Followers of Imām al-Mahdī (ʿaj)

Once we come to love the Imām of our time, we will naturally want to be among his helpers and will yearn for his reappearance. Our living Imām is waiting for us, as a community, to be at a stage where we are ready for his return. Narrations such as the following indicate that if we have maʿrifah of Imām al-Mahdī's status, we will be able to recognize how he is amongst us day and night.

Imām Jaʿfar aṣ-Ṣādiq (ʿa) said, "For the Qāʾim there are two ghaybahs: One of them is short, and the other is long. In the first ghaybah, only the elite of his Shi'ah will know of his location. And in the second, none except the elite among the followers in their practice of religion will know of it."

As this narration indicates, during the first and minor occultation, the Imām had appointed four specific individuals as his representatives over the period of 69 years of this occultation. After this, the Imām began his second and major occultation. During this time, there are some elite people who may communicate with the Imām through various means, but we do not specifically know who these individuals are, and they usually do not make these communications public.

The time of the major occultation is a challenging time, but one that holds within it a great opportunity too. The narrations indicate that those who believe in the Imām in this difficult period of occultation, and who actively anticipate his reappearance, have a very special status with Allah (swt), and are in fact the best of people:

> "The people of the time of the occultation of al-Qāi'm, who believe in his Imāmah and who await his reappearance are better than the people of all other times. This is because Allah, the Blessed and Exalted, gave them such strong belief and understanding that the occultation became to them like seeing, and made them in that time to have the status of those who fought alongside the Messenger of Allah (ṣ) with the sword. They are the truly sincere and the true Shīʿah and the callers to the religion of Allah, the Glorified, the Exalted, both in public and private."

So, how can we become his true followers?

According to the narrations, the followers of Imām al-Mahdī (ʿaj) are devout by night and lions by day.

This means that they are active in the day, standing up against oppression and dishonesty while fulfilling their obligations to their family, community and society. At night, they humble themselves in prayer seeking nearness to Allah (swt).

They are courageous, determined, and submissive on Allah's path while being patient and wise in their struggle for Islamic values being expanded throughout the world. Patience is one of their characteristics; they are never hasty. They are wise and patient in their struggle for Islamic values to be spread throughout the world.

Let us now look at the features of these blessed people, the followers of Imām al-Mahdī (ʿaj), described in some narrations:

"The nature of his (al-Mahdī's) followers will be pure and immaculate. They will be free from hypocrisy and all other contaminations."

"Their (al-Mahdī's followers') hearts will be untainted and unadulterated by malice, jealousy and enmity."

Gaining closeness and love of the Imām will help us get closer to Allah (swt), and so it is important that we understand what it will mean for him to reappear and our role as people of the end of times. Our responsibility as we strive to be these people is to do Intiẓār of the Imām and act in a way that if he were to come tomorrow, we would be prepared.

THE HEREAFTER: AFTER WE DIE, WE WILL BE BROUGHT BACK TO LIFE AND FACE THE CONSEQUENCES OF OUR ACTIONS

Section 7- Maʿād

7.1

THE SOUL

The last of the five fundamental beliefs of Islam is the Resurrection (al-Maʿād). We would have no access to the details about the Resurrection without the Qurʾān and the Noble Prophet (s). While some of the general concepts can be proven by our intellects, the details must be obtained through the scripture.

In Islam, unlike in other faiths, the emphasis on Resurrection is so great that over 25% or 1,640 āyāt [1] of the Qurʾān refer to it. It is a fundamental part of the belief in the Unity of God [2], the selection of Prophets {38:46-47}, self-purification {79:39-41}, staying on the right path 38:26}, piety, worshipping, peace of mind, bravery, and justice. Denying the existence of the Hereafter can lead to social and economic crimes {83:1-5} [3], a sinful life [7], immoral behaviour {75:5-6}, etc.

The soul is one of the important concepts that is related to the Resurrection and the Hereafter, and it is the focus of the rest of this lesson. Allah (swt), the All-Wise, has created us with a body (our physical existence) and a soul (our spiritual existence). Allah (swt) tells us in the Noble Qur'ān that He creates our physical existence but also brings to life within us a different type of creation. This different creation is our soul, or our immaterial (non-physical) existence.

[1] Sheikh Mansour Leghaei, Journey to the Unseen World, Lesson 1

[2] Repeated 30 times in the Qurʾān is the concept of belief in Allah resulting in a belief in the hereafter

[3] concept of the Gyges Ring (http://en.wikipedia.org/wiki/Ring_of_Gyges or the Harry Potters 'Cloak of Invisibility' whereby if one is not caught, one can get away with anything or whether a typical person would be moral if he did not have to fear the consequences of his actions)

"Then We created the drop of fluid as a clinging mass. Then We created the clinging mass as a fleshy tissue. Then We created the fleshy tissue as bones. Then We clothed the bones with flesh. Then We brought him to life as a different creation. So blessed is Allah, the best of creators!" {23:14}

Understanding our soul will lead us to understanding Allah (swt). We also believe that some of our journey in the afterlife is carried out through the soul, in a process or place called barzakh. The soul will then be reunited with the body during resurrection. Imam ʿAlī (ʿa) says:

من عرف نفسه عرف ربه

"One who attains inner knowledge of his soul attains inner knowledge of his Lord." [1]

What is the soul and how do we know it exists?

The soul is the reality of who we are. Our soul goes beyond our physical body (which is material, because it consists of matter), as it lies in the immaterial, or non-physical spiritual realm. In the Qur'ān, Allah (swt) describes the stages of the creation of the fetus physically, but when he comes to the creation of the soul He says:

"And then (We) produced it as another creation." {23:14}

This confirms that the soul goes beyond the physical realm into the immaterial (non-physical) realm of creation.

The Noble Qur'ān also describes the soul as being from the command (amr) of Allah (swt).

[1] Mizānl ul-Hikmah, Hadīth #4065

"They will ask you concerning the soul (rūh). Say: the soul is from the Command of my Lord." {17:85}

This expression of "the Command of Allah" relates to another āyah as well.

"Surely, His Command (amr) is that when He intends a thing, is only that He says to it: 'Be' and it is." {36:82}

According to one interpretation, when Allah (swt) refers to the soul being from His Command, He is referring to the Command of existence. In other words, the soul is what gives something "life" and "spirit".

This is why we learned in Grade 7 that the soul is what makes 'me' me, such that if we were to think of ourselves without being distracted, we would find our soul.

We all have an intuitive knowledge of the existence of our soul so there is no need to prove its existence. However, there are some arguments that alert us to the existence of the soul.

Scientifically, we know that the physical body we have now is not what we had in the past or will have in the future because most of the cells in our body are constantly dying and regenerating (every 7-9 years). Despite this, we still identify ourselves as 'me'!

When we refer to our limbs we say, "my arm" or "my leg" and even though they are part of our bodies, we know they are not 'me'. Instinctively, we also know that our body parts in and of themselves do not have an identity of their own. For example, my arm only has an identity because of me, not on its own - yet I am not my arm, nor any other part of my body! Similarly, we refer to the 'body' of a deceased person because we instinctively know that upon death, the soul is separated from the body and therefore we cannot refer to the dead body as a person.

Other phenomena such as dreams and near death experiences further highlight the presence of the soul.

Spiritual Development

Just as we grow physically through our life and grow bigger and more mature over time, we are also supposed to develop spiritually. Our spiritual development is even more important than our physical development. The soul goes through a number of stages in order to develop and reach its perfection. According to Islamic teachings, the soul has three stages of development, from the lowest to the most perfect.

01.

The Evil-Commanding Soul (al-Nafs al-Ammārah

وَمَا أُبَرِّئُ نَفْسِي ۚ إِنَّ النَّفْسَ لَأَمَّارَةٌ بِالسُّوءِ إِلَّا مَا رَحِمَ رَبِّي ۚ إِنَّ رَبِّي غَفُورٌ رَحِيمٌ

"Yet I do not absolve my [own carnal] soul, for the [carnal] soul indeed prompts [men] to evil, except inasmuch as my Lord has mercy. Indeed my Lord is all-forgiving, all-merciful.' {12:53}

Allah (swt) has placed within us certain emotions like anger and lust. These emotions are necessary for our survival. However, they must be controlled and limited by our intellect.

Otherwise, if not checked and controlled, our desires go beyond the limits of being beneficial for us and instead command us to do evil. This aspect of our soul can eventually overpower us and cause us physical and spiritual harm if we don't work to control it.

02.

The Blaming Soul (an-Nafs al-Lawwāmah)

وَلَا أُقْسِمُ بِالنَّفْسِ اللَّوَّامَةِ

"And I swear by the self-critical soul!" {75:2}

The reproaching (blaming) soul, often called the conscience, is the aspect of the soul that judges our actions using the standard of our pure fitṛah. If the actions go against our fitṛah and what is good for the soul, it makes us feel guilty. If the actions are in line with our pure fitṛah, it gives a feeling of peace and tranquility.

Once a man came to the Noble Prophet (s) to ask a question. Before he spoke, the Noble Prophet (s) said to him: "Do you wish to ask your question or should I tell you what your question is?"

The man was surprised and asked the Prophet (s) to reveal the question. The Noble Prophet (s) replied: "You have come to ask about what is good (virtue) and what is bad (vice)."

That was in fact exactly what the man had come to ask!

The Noble Prophet (s) placed his fingertips on the man's heart and said:

"Check it with your heart, regardless of what people may say; righteousness is what your soul (nafs) is at rest with whilst vice is the action after whose performance you feel guilty." [1]

In order to understand what is good and bad, we have to learn Islamic rules and guidelines. We can't simply rely on our gut feelings to understand what is good and what is evil for our soul. However, this hadīth teaches us that for sincere and pure people, doing acts of goodness can bring tranquility to their soul, whereas even the thought of doing evil can disturb them.

[1] Shahīd Mutạhharī, Āshnāyī ba Qur'ān, Vol. 1, P. 74; Musnad of Ahṃad ibn Hạnbal (17545)

03.

The Tranquil Soul (an-Nafs al-Muṭma'innah)

"O soul that art at rest! Return to your Lord, well-pleased (with Him), well-pleasing (Him), So enter among My servants, and enter into My garden." {89:27-30}

This is the stage the soul reaches when a person has managed to firmly control their desires and to take heed of their conscience. In other words, they have learned to manage the "commands" of the aspect of the soul that is concerned with emotions and desires and they have taken heed of the warnings of the self-critical soul and improved their character and actions.

The ultimate reward for having achieved this is that Allah (swt) accommodates the person in a special place in paradise!

How do we tame our commanding soul?

Before we begin this section, it has to be noted that the aim of a Muslim is not to kill their desires but to control or tame them, so that instead of the desires controlling the person, the person controls their desires. For example, instead of my desire telling me what and when to eat, I tell it when and what to eat. But I do still need to eat, and if I don't provide nourishment to my body, I am misusing the trust Allah has given me. Imam ʿAlī (ʿa) says:

"Rule your souls by continuously struggling with them." [1]

As alluded to earlier, the most effective way of taming the soul is to struggle with oneself (or in other words, the commanding soul). This struggle (or jihād) is considered the greatest struggle of all. Allah (swt) tells us in the Noble Qurʾān:

"And the soul and Him Who made it perfect, Then He inspired it to understand what is right and wrong for it; He will indeed be successful who purifies it, And he will indeed fail who corrupts it." {91:7-10}

Imam ʿAlī (ʿa) says,

"One who does not refine his soul will be disgraced by bad habits." [2]

Imam Jaʿfar as-Ṣādiq (a) said in regards to a particularly difficult battle fought during the life of the Prophet (s):

"The Prophet (ṣ) of God dispatched a contingent of the army (to the battlefront). Upon their (successful) return, he (s) said: 'Blessed are those who have performed the minor jihād and have yet to perform the major jihād.' When asked, 'What is the major jihād?' the Prophet (ṣ) replied: 'The jihād of the self (struggle against self).'" [3]

[1] Scale of Wisdom - tradition 6195

[2] Scale of wisdom - tradition 6199

[3] Bihar al-Anwar, Vol. 19, p. 182, Hadīth # 31 (from an article http://www.al-islam.org/nutshell/merits_soul/)

This struggle is considered as the major struggle (al-jihād al-akbar) as it is much more difficult than fighting in the battlefield. In the struggle against the self, one has to constantly battle enemies that are hosted inside his own existence and this struggle lasts a lifetime.

When we study or learn about akhlāq, we are learning how to train our soul and move towards our spiritual perfection. When we study aḥkām and the rules of Islam, we are also learning about actions that harm our soul (ḥarām and makrūh acts) and actions that help our soul (wājib and mustaḥab actions).

At the time of our death, our bodies will decay and be absorbed into the earth. However, our soul remains alive and enters the world of Barzakh, where it may remain for thousands of years. During this time, as well as on Resurrection Day, our fate will be determined by the level of perfection that our soul reaches. Therefore, just as we look after the physical health of our body to live a healthy life in this world, we should look after the spiritual health of our souls which determines our fate for eternity.

7.2

DEATH

Death is an inescapable reality. Regardless of whether we are believers or not, each of us accepts death as a fact of our existence. Since it is inescapable, and there is some mystery around it, there are some questions we naturally begin to ask. What is death? Is it destruction, annihilation, and non-existence? Or is it a change, a development, and a transition from one world to another? In this lesson, we will have an understanding of the main Islamic beliefs about death and the importance of preparing ourselves for this journey.

What is Death?

Death, in essence, is the separation of the soul from the body. It occurs when the soul leaves the body. The body dies, remains in this material world, and decomposes, while the soul moves on to the next stage of its existence.

Therefore, death is not the absence of life. Rather just like life, 'death' is something which is created, and is itself a stage of life. Allah (swt), the Exalted says in the Qur'ān:

"Blessed be He... who has created death and life, so that He might test you which of you is most righteous in action" {67:1-2}

Death is a continuation of the life of the soul, a transition from one abode, this temporary world, to an eternal life. Imām Ḥasan (ʿa) said:

"(Death is) the greatest happiness that comes to the believers, when they migrate from the house of misery to the eternal bliss; and (it is) the greatest disaster that befalls the unbelievers, when they go from their paradise (i.e. this world) to the fire which will never be extinguished and will never burn itself out!"

[1] Day of Judgment, by Allamah Sayyid Saeed Akhtar Rizvi, P. 22

Reasons for Death

There are many reasons why death is a necessary part of the journey for every living creature, whether it is a plant, animal, or even human being.

1. One of the basic rules of creation in this material world is that it is not possible for life in the physical world to continue forever. This is because, generally speaking, for one creature to live, another must die. For example, for a lion to live, a gazelle must die, or for a goat to live, it must eat grass, and so on.
2. Death is a movement from one world to another: a world in which we are judged and rewarded for our choices.
3. Human beings were not created to live in this world forever. We came here only to learn and act. Death in this life is like our graduation from school where we are now ready to step into real life.

The Last moments before Death

We have learned that death is a movement from one world to another. This transition is difficult for the human soul. Just as the birth of a baby into this world involves a lot of pain and the baby emerges crying, the movement from this world to the next involves pain and difficulty as well. The Noble Qur'ān refers to these last moments that come before death as "the stupor of death."

"And the stupor of death will come in truth; that is what you were trying to escape." {50:19}

This is a difficult time. For most people, it will involve both physical and spiritual pain. A person begins to lose their ability to speak or act in any way. Those who squandered Allah's blessings and did not repent for their misdeeds will truly begin to regret much of what they did in their lives. They will wish that they had spent their time chasing after what they could take with them to their next life (good deeds that lead to a pure soul) rather than what they are going to leave behind (wealth, prestige, and worldly comforts).

Remembrance of Death

We will learn in later lessons that whatever happens to us after our death is a direct result of what we did in this world. Whatever happiness or suffering our soul will experience in its next life is a consequence of what we do here. Therefore, it becomes imperative that we constantly remember death. Through remembering that this may occur at any moment we begin to be more aware of the need to make good choices and prepare for what comes after death. Imām ʿAlī (ʿa) said to his son Imām al-Ḥasan (ʿa): "Enliven your heart by preaching...make it humble by remembering death, make it believe in mortality...recall what befell those who came before you...You will find that they departed and lodged in a lonely house..." [1]

When remembering death, we should remember how its mysteries and suddenness:

1. **Location**: Where we die is unknown to us: "...and no one knows in what land he shall die; surely Allah is Knowing, Aware..." {31:34}
2. **Time**: When we die is also known to us: "What! Do the people of the towns then feel secure from Our punishment coming to them by night while they sleep? What! Do the people of the towns feel secure from Our punishment coming to them in the morning while they play?" {7:97-98}
3. **State**: We hope that we will die in a good state of being dutiful servants of Allah! "...therefore die not unless you are Muslims!" {2:132}

Observance of our Actions

When we remember the suddenness of death, we become more aware of the importance of our actions, and the need to improve ourselves.

Maintaining consistency in reflecting on our actions can be a difficult task but remembering certain things can help us.. How we were last year doesn't matter, but rather, how we are when we die. If we were very pious last year, but now have lost our faith, we will be coming to Allah (swt) as a disbeliever, regardless of our past. We must ensure that we are keeping up our good deeds and staying away from evil deeds regularly. This can happen when we remember that death is not a stranger that will come knocking at our doors only when we are 90 years old or older. It is a reality that can happen at any time!

[1] Nahj al-Balāghah, Letter # 31

A good example of this is of a man during the time of the Prophet (s) who, after hearing the message of the Prophet, began to accept Islam. However, thinking he couldn't quit alcohol and had plenty of time, he decided that he would continue drinking for another year and then accept Islam. Unfortunately, he died before the end of the year and met his Lord as a disbeliever.

Steps of Observance and Accounting

يَا أَيُّهَا الَّذِينَ آمَنُوا اتَّقُوا اللَّهَ وَلْتَنظُرْ نَفْسٌ مَا قَدَّمَتْ لِغَدٍ ۖ وَاتَّقُوا اللَّهَ ۚ إِنَّ اللَّهَ خَبِيرٌ بِمَا تَعْمَلُونَ {18}وَلَا تَكُونُوا كَالَّذِينَ نَسُوا اللَّهَ فَأَنسَاهُمْ أَنفُسَهُمْ ۚ أُولَٰئِكَ هُمُ الْفَاسِقُونَ {19}

O you who believe! be careful of (your duty to) Allah, and let every soul consider what it has sent on for its tomorrow, and be careful of (your duty to) Allah; surely Allah is Aware of what you do. And be not like those who became oblivious of Allah, so He made them oblivious of their own souls: these it is that are the transgressors. {59:18-19}

Imagine you are a student in class and each term your teacher comes to check that you have completed all the tasks that they have set for you throughout the term. If you have carefully kept an account of all of the tasks given, those completed and those not completed, when your teacher announces that she wants to check if you have kept your work up to date, you wouldn't have anything to worry about. On the other hand, the student who has not kept his work up to date will panic when the teacher comes around to check everyone's work. Death is like this, because it can come at any time.

This is the same for our deeds and actions. If we do not keep a track of our actions and reflect on them, we will not be aware of our sins and mistakes, and we will not give ourselves a chance to improve. It is necessary for a Muslim to habitually review their actions on a regular basis and assess themselves objectively. Besides reflecting on our actions on a daily basis, we should also use certain milestones like birthdays, new calendar years, and other special Islamic occasions to think about our spiritual progress over the last month or year.

The Prophet (s) says in his will to his close companion Abū Dharr:

"O Abū Dharr, no one can be from the pious people unless he keeps an account of his actions: what you have done, eaten, and said today." [1]

Imām Mūsā al-Kāzịm (ʿa) said:

"One who does not examine and evaluate himself every day is not one of us. (A person who examines himself), if he does a good deed, he beseeches God to increase him (in virtues) and if he has perpetrated a vice, he seeks God's forgiveness for it and is penitent before Him." [2]

The person who is going to his Lord should be aware of his actions. This is the reason we should observe our actions each and every day. Self-observance and accounting can be divided into four stages:

1. **Al-Mushāratạh**: Impose some conditions on yourself that today you will do certain things and that if you do not do them, you will implement certain consequences.
    - Eg. a person who has the habit of lying puts a condition on themselves that they will not lie today. If they lie, the consequence will be that they will deny themselves a particular pleasure (e.g. not playing video games for two days).
2. **Al-Murāqabah**: Observing yourself and being conscious of the conditions you set on yourself at the beginning of that day.
3. **Al-Muhạsabah**: At the end of the day or time period, make yourself accountable for your actions.
    - Eg. A person looks back at their day and checks whether they lied or not during that day.
4. **Al-Muʿātabah/Al-Muʿāqabah**: applying the consequences of breaking the conditions set at the beginning of the day.
    - If they lied, they apply the consequences they set for themselves. If they did not, then they thank Allah (swt) for this and pray to continue their success.

[1] Wasāʾil ash-Shīʿah, Vol. 16, P. 98

[2] Al-Kāfī, Vol. 2, Kitāb al-Īmān wal-Kufr, Bāb Muhạsabāt al-Aʿmāl, Hạdīth No. 2

Allah (swt) loves His servant who is increasing in nearness to Him. Therefore, one shouldn't stay in the same state that they have been in for years and not attempt to increase and multiply their good actions. For example, if one wakes up for Fajr every morning, but does so towards the end of its time, they can work to wake up for Fajr at the beginning of its time. Or if someone wakes up for Fajr at the beginning of its time, they can work to stay up until sunrise. That way we are continuously working to improve ourselves.

At the same time, while our actions are increasing in number, many of us may fall into the trap of feeling proud over our good deeds. It is always important to recognize that any good action is a blessing from Allah (swt) because He has guided us toward this.

7.3- Barzakh

BARZAKH

The dissociation between the body and the soul is called death. As soon as we die, the soul enters the stage of Barzakh which literally means a 'barrier' between two things. In other words, it means that Allah (swt) has placed a curtain or an intermediary stage between this world and the Hereafter. The world of Barzakh is often referred to as "the grave" in the ḥadīth. So when we speak about something happening to a soul in the grave, we are talking about this happening in Barzakh. Barzakh is followed by the Day of Resurrection. Everyone who has died so far, good or evil, old or young is currently in Barzakh. They are either enjoying a taste of paradise, suffering temporary punishment, or are in a lengthy state of slumber. All of them are 'waiting' for the Day of Judgment.

The characteristics of the life in Barzakh include:

- The pressure of the grave, which is a special punishment for specific sins
- Being able to hear the people still alive in this world without being able to reply
- Being questioned about our actions
- Being able to visit loved ones in this world

We will now examine each of these characteristics in more detail.

Characteristics of Barzakh: Questioning

One of the aspects of life in Barzakh is that people are questioned in the grave. People will be asked about their Creator, Prophet, Imām, religion, scripture, life, youth, and wealth.

Imām aṣ-Ṣādiq (ʿa) said,

"A deceased will be asked in his grave about five things: his ṣalāh, his zakāt, his Ḥajj, his fasting, and his wilāyah (love and obedience to Ahl al-Bayt). Then the wilāyah says to the other four from the side of the grave: "Whatever you are short of I will complete it (for him)." [1]

[1] Al-Kāfī, Vol 3, P. 241

When a person is buried in the grave, two angels will confront them asking about their beliefs and all that they have done. It should be noted that grave, in this terminology, does not merely mean a pit in which a dead body is buried. The word "grave" in Islamic literature is another expression for Barzakh. Imām as-Ṣādiq (ʿa) said:

"The Barzakh is the 'grave' and it is the reward or punishment between this world and the Hereafter." [1]

Also, questions and answers are not a matter of the tongue. We will be questioned of the reality of our belief and the answers come from the inner voice. In other words, mere knowledge will be of no use if it is not combined with belief and action.

Pressure of the Grave

This is a type of punishment which varies for different people. It means the soul of a dead person will be under a type of pressure as a means of torturing to cleanse the soul.The narrations indicate that most people, including many believers, will suffer the punishment of pressure in the grave [2]. There are however also some narrations that indicate that performing certain good actions consistently such as night-prayers, fasting, Hajj can protect a person from the pressure of the grave. [3]) There are particular actions that cause this type of punishment.

The story of Saʿd ibn Muʿādh tells us a little about the pressure of the grave. Saʿd was one of the leaders of the Muslims and among the closest people to the Prophet (s). Unfortunately, Sa'd was wounded severely by an arrow during the Battle of Aḥzāb and passed away soon afterwards. During his funeral procession, the Prophet (s) carried different corners of his coffin, moving from one corner to the next, as a mark of great respect for him. The Prophet (s) even said there were many angels who had come to join the procession of Saʿd. When they reached the graveyard, the Prophet (s) himself entered the grave and prepared it for Saʿd. When Saʿd's mother saw all this, she was very happy and congratulated her son. However, the Prophet (s) said that it was too soon to speak, because Saʿd would likely suffer the pressure of the grave.

[1] Biḥār al-Anwār, Vol. 6, P. 218
[2] Al-Kāfi, 3:136
[3] Al-Faqīh, 2:139
[4] ʿIlal al-Sharāʿi, Vol. 1, P. 309; Biḥār al-Anwār, Vol. 6, P. 220

When asked why this would happen even though the Prophet (s) had so much respect for him and he was such a great man, the Prophet (s) responded, "He was ill-mannered with his family." [4]

We can see from this story that the pressure of the grave is often a way for Allah (swt) to purify people from some of their sins before the Hereafter. Even though Saʿd was a great person, he would still face difficulty in the grave because of his ill manners towards his family, and this would hopefully purify him and save him from punishment on Judgment Day.

Visitation of the Souls and Benefiting from the Living Ones

Depending on the status of the souls, they may be able to visit their families. If it is the soul of a believer, they will be shown only the good actions of his or her family. The soul of a non-believer will be shown the bad actions of his or her family. This is another type of reward or punishment in Barzakh. It is narrated from the Noble Prophet (s) that the departed souls visit their homes every Friday and call out:

"O people of my house! May Allah bless you! Have mercy on us! Whatever we have done in this world, we are facing its consequences now while the fruits of our hard work (in the world) are being enjoyed by others. Favor us by giving on our behalf a dirham, or bread, or clothes (to the needy), so that Allah may reward you with heavenly attire." [1]

It is very important that we should not forget our dead, especially our parents! They have no power to perform good deeds in their current state, and they rely on their children, relatives, and other close ones to aid them with good deeds. They eagerly await the favors. We should particularly pray for them in Ṣalāt ul-Layl but also after every prayer. We should also try to share the reward of any good actions we do with our deceased relatives. Dedicating the reward to them does not mean we will lose out on any of the reward ourselves. In this world, if we share something with someone, we lose a part of it. However, in the world after death, sharing the rewards of an action does not diminish from the rewards of the one who performed the action, but rather increases them!

[1] Wasāʾil ash-Shīʿah, Vol. 2 P. 223

Hearing without Reply

The dead, during their status in Barzakh, can hear when we communicate with them, although they are unable to respond. Or, in the cases of the special intimate servants of Allah, they do respond, but we cannot hear their response.

Several cases of the Prophets and Imāms talking to the dead have been recorded. After the battle of Badr, the Prophet (s) addressed the dead soldiers from the troops of Quraysh and spoke to them. Similarly, Imām 'Alī (ʿa) sat down next to the corpses of Kaʿb ibn Suwar and Ṭalḥah after the Battle of Jamal—the camel—and said to them:

"Surely, I found the promise of my Lord to be true, so did you find the promise of your Lord true too?" [1]

Preparing for Barzakh

Different sins result in varying severities and types of punishments in the grave. Abū Dharr, the pious and truthful companion of the prophet, when burying his son was saddened that his son was no longer with him, and he prayed for him at his graveside. Often, when a child dies before his mother or father, his parents would have unhesitatingly wished that they had left this world before the child. However, due to Abū Dharr's knowledge, he said to his son at that moment that he would have preferred to die instead of his son had it not been for his fear of the punishment of the grave. [2]

At the same time, for the virtuous servants of Allah (swt), unimaginable bounties and pleasures in Barzakh have been promised. The extent to which we enjoy or suffer in the grave depends entirely on what we have done in this life.

[1] Sharh, Nahj al-Balāghah, Ibn Abil-Ḥadid, Vol. 1, P. 248

[2] Muntahā al-Āmāl, P. 296

7.4- The Resurrection

In the previous lessons, we have discussed various aspects of life after this world, from death to Barzakh. In this lesson, we shall discuss one of the fundamental beliefs of all major religions, especially Islam: Maʿād or Resurrection. As we have learned in previous years, there are many names for the Day of Resurrection (Yawm ad-Dīn, Yawm al-Qiyāmah, Yawm al-Ḥashr, Yawm al-Ḥisāb, etc.). It should be noted that 'yawm' or 'day' in this context does not mean the regular day (24 hours), but rather to a period of time which is not describable with the measure of time as we know today. This is why the Qur'ān uses a very large time span, such as one thousand years, to describe it [1]. The other possible reason for why it is called 'day' is because, just like the sun exposes everything, the 'light' of truth will expose the reality of our actions. [2]

LOGICAL ARGUMENTS FOR THE DAY OF RESURRECTION

We know that the Day of Resurrection will definitely take place because the Qur'ān, just like the divinely-sent books before it, speaks about it as a definite occurrence. Prophet Muḥammad (s) explained in detail what will take place on the Day of Judgment. But is there a way for us to be convinced about the need of the Day of Resurrection through local reasoning? We will now look at three logical arguments that can be used to demonstrate the existence of the Day of Resurrection.

[1] Noble Qur'ān, Sūrah as-Sajdah (32), Verse 5; Noble Qur'ān, Sūrah al-Maʿārij (70), Verse 5

[2] The Hereafter (Maʿad)- Āyatullāh Dastaghaib Shirazi, P. 64, "How will the Powdered Bones Become Alive?"; Noble Qur'ān, Sūrah az-Zumar (39), Verse 47

01.

The Argument from Innate Knowledge

Human beings are born with some characteristics already pre-programmed in us. These characteristics are called innate characteristics. Some of these include hunger, thirst, love, etc. and, as Allah (swt), the Almighty, has pre-programmed these things in us, He has also created legitimate and good ways to fulfill them. Loving immortality and the attribute of survival after death is a natural desire of mankind that appears to have been held by human beings from the earliest of times. The instinct of immortality will not be satisfied unless there is an immortal life after this mortal one.

Creating an innate characteristic and not allowing it to be fulfilled would be in vain and incongruent with divine wisdom. Therefore, Allah must definitely create a realm (the Hereafter) where we can live forever.

02.

Argument from Wisdom [1]

We are living in a meaningful world in which everything has a purpose and an aim. If death were the end of everything, the creation of the entire universe would be in vain (without purpose). We can all see that we live in a vast and expansive universe, the limits of which we still have not discovered. We can also see the incredible level of detail and precision within this universe, and how it has been designed to permit life in general, and human life in particular. It does not make sense that all this is here so that one day it would just perish and cease to exist, with no consequences or effects. Why would the Wise and Intelligent Creator, Allah (swt), create such an incredible world in vain (without a purpose or reason that comes after it)? Allah (swt) asks us to consider this question many times in the Qur'ān, and affirms that this world was not created in vain.

[1] Noble Qur'ān, Sūrah al-Hijr (15), Verse 85; Noble Qur'ān, Sūrah al-Mu'minūn (23), Verse 115

"...those who reflect on the creations of the skies and the Earth (thinking): "Our Nurturer, You have not created this in vain, Glory to be You so protect us from the punishment of the Fire." {3:191}

03.

Argument from Justice

Justice is one of God's attributes as mentioned in the previous lessons. The whole universe is created according to the principle of justice. However, the history of man presented many criminals that never received their full punishment in this world. How many innocent people are killed without their murderers found? How many properties are stolen and the thieves never caught? Therefore, there must be a great day of judgment in which all tyrants, oppressors, and criminals will be judged with true justice.

The Resurrection

Islam has put very great emphasis on the concept of the Day of Judgement and the Hereafter. Maʿād means the return and the re-joining of scattered particles and the joining of the soul to the body after their separation. Maʿād therefore does not mean that Allah (swt) brings something out of non-existence. The question then arises: how will Allah (swt) bring us to life after our body has completely disintegrated?

Once a man called Ibn Abī Khalaf came to the Noble Prophet (s) with an old bone in his hand. He was pressing and crushing it with his hand. When it all became powder, he blew it off his hands with his mouth and asked, "Who will make this stuff alive?"

It was then that a verse was revealed to the Noble Prophet (s):

"And he strikes out a likeness for Us and forgets his own creation. Says he: Who will give life to the bones when they are rotten? Say: He will give life to them Who brought them into existence at first, and He is cognizant of all creation."

Stages of the Day of Resurrection

The Noble Prophet (s) described the Resurrection Day as follows. ʿAmr b. Mʿadī was one of the most famous brave and courageous warriors among Arabs. Once, when he was a polytheist, he visited the Noble Prophet (s). The Prophet (s) invited him to Islam, and said: "If you believe in Islam, God Almighty will protect you from the greatest fright on the Day of Resurrection."

ʿAmr asked, "O Muḥammad! What is the great fright? I am so tough-hearted that nothing can frighten me."

The Noble Prophet (s) said: "O ʿAmr! It is not so, as you imagined. It will be a tremendously frightening sound, which will make all the dead alive and make the entire living die, except those whom Allah (swt) wishes that they should not die. Then again there will be a terrible roar which will make all the dead stand and line up. The sky will be fragmented. All the mountains will break up and become scattered. Thus there will be no living being whose heart will not be palpating due to fear, remembering the sins committed by it. All will be worrying only about their own selves except those whom Allah (swt) wills (that they may not become restless)." [2]

ʿAmr eventually became a Muslim and demonstrated his warrior skills as part of the Muslim army.

The Blowing of the Trumpet

We learn from the Holy Qur'ān that the first thing that will happen on the Day of Resurrection is the blowing of the trumpet (by the angel Isrāfīl) [3]. Every living thing will die (except those whom Allah (swt) wishes). All the remaining humans shall die and also experience Barzakh.

[1] Noble Qurʿān, Sūrah Yāsīn (36), Verses 78-79; Tafsīr Nemūneh, Vol. 18, P. 480

[2] Kashf al-Ghummah, P. 228

[3] Noble Qur'ān, Sūrah az-Zumar (39), Verse 68; Noble Qur'ān, Sūrah an-Naml (27), Verse 87

Once all the souls have been taken, the Angel of Death will come to God to report this and Allah (swt) will command that even the Angel of Death should die! The second trumpet will be blown and everyone will come back to life.

The Rising from the Grave

One day, the angel Jibrāīl came to the Noble Prophet (s) and asked, "Would you like to observe the condition of people on the Day of Resurrection?"

"Yes," the Prophet replied. Jibrāīl, the trustworthy angel, took the Noble Prophet (s) to the graveyard of Baqī" (Medina). He shook a grave and said, "Get up at the order of your Lord." The grave split at once and a man with a radiant face raised his head from the grave saying: '(All) praise is due to Allah (swt), Who has made good to us His promise' {39:74}.

Thereafter, he shook another grave and said, "Rise up at the command of your Lord." At once, another man with a very ugly and frightened face came out of this grave and said: 'O woe to us!' Jibrāīl said, "The faithful and the unbelievers will rise up from their graves in this condition." [1]

Assembly on the field of Maḥshar (the Resurrection)

Upon rising from their graves, everyone will be astonished at the sight before them. Fear then will set in, such fear that they will wish to flee from the scene and Allah (swt) says that they will be like **'scattered moths,'** {101:4} or '**scattered locusts**.' {54:7}

On that day, everyone will try to hide themselves from each other; fathers and mothers will flee from their own children! Their running away will be of no use. Those who had any connection with God in this world will flee to Allah (swt) whereas for others there will be no escape.

Realizing that there is no way out, they will ask each other for their share of good deeds but no one will help as they will need whatever they have! It is for the fear of this day that we should gather as many good deeds as we can for ourselves and develop a strong relationship with the Ahl al-Bayt (ʿa) as nothing else will avail us then.

[1] The Hereafter (Ma'ad)- Ayatollah Dastaghaib Shirazi, P. 77 "How will they Raise their Heads from Graves?"

Book of Actions

Soon after, every individual shall be handed their Book of Actions. In general, the Book of Actions is something that each and every individual or each nation will carry with them which consists of their entire actions in this world, good or bad. Every single action, word or in some cases thought will be recorded. Allah (swt) says:

"He utters not a word but there is by him a watcher at hand." {50:18}

A man once asked the Imām (ʿa) how angels know the good intention of a faithful person? The Imām (ʿa) replied: "As soon as a servant thinks of doing a good deed, his body emanates a pleasing fragrance. So the angels understand it and they record that good intention. When someone thinks of committing an evil, the bad smell of it hurts the angels. If a man thinks of doing good, a good is at once noted in his record of deeds. Then, if he carries out that good deed, ten goods are noted in his record." [1]

On the Day of Resurrection, every soul shall read its Book of Actions. The book will be handed over to its author, i.e. the doer. Once you look at your book, every single action accompanied with its real intention is precisely and accurately engraved in the book. It will be the most comprehensive biography ever of the person's life. It contains the entire life of the person, from cradle to the grave. For some,

"...because of what is recorded therein, they will say: Ah! Woe to us! What a book this is! It leaves out nothing small or great, but takes account thereof." {18:49}

We have learned in previous years that this book is not like a book we know of in this world. It will be a record of our deeds such that even our limbs will testify to our actions!

Those who believed and did good in this world will be given their book in their right hand. They will be happy and relieved. They will say:

[1] The Hereafter (Ma'ad)- Ayatollah Dastaghaib Shirazi, P. 83, "The Fragrance of Good Intention Alerts the Angels"

"Surely I knew I shall meet my account. So he shall be in a life of pleasure." {19:69}

The sinners shall be given their book of actions in their left hand. They will be ashamed and will say:

"O would that my book had never been given to me! And I had not known what my account was! O would that it had made an end (of me). My wealth has availed me of nothing, and my authority has gone away from me." {69:25-29}

Questioning

Before being allowed to proceed through to the Sirāt, everyone will be questioned about how they used the bounties and gifts they were given in this world, and particularly, how they used their life. The questions will include:

1. How did you spend your life and in which deeds were you engaged with when you were young?
2. From where and how did you earn money? Where and how did you spend it?

There will also be questioning about the wilāyah and obedience toward Prophet Muhammad (s) and his progeny.

The Transience of This World and the Eternity of the Hereafter

We have been put in this world to gather as much provision as we can for that day. The period of time we spend in this world is very short when compared to the Hereafter. Allah says in the Noble Qur'ān:

وَمَا الْحَيَاةُ الدُّنْيَا إِلاَّ لَعِبٌ وَلَهْوٌ وَلَلدَّارُ الآخِرَةُ خَيْرٌ لِّلَّذِينَ يَتَّقُونَ أَفَلاَ تَعْقِلُونَ

"And this world's life is naught but a play and an idle sport and certainly the abode of the hereafter is better for those who guard (against evil); do you not then understand?" {6:32}

One of the primary causes of punishment and suffering in the Hereafter is the love for this world. We can easily forget about the Hereafter and focus only on the temporary pleasures of this world. In order to be successful both in this world and the Hereafter, we have to detach ourselves from this world and understand that everything we have belongs to Allah (swt). We need to use the bounties given to us by Allah (swt) to purchase a place in Heaven in the Hereafter. This means that we should spend our energy, money, and time to obtain everlasting pleasures in the Hereafter, rather than wasting these on the temporary pleasures of this world. Imām ʿAlī (ʿa) also has said:

"One who chases after this world, it will evade him. Whilst if one does not actively seek after it, it will come towards him. If one sees through it, then it will bestow him with insight, whilst if one looks at it (in and of itself) then it will blind him." [1]

We can do this by:

1. Shortening our wishes and desires for this world
2. Appreciating every blessing
3. Abstaining from ḥarām
4. Not being preoccupied in what other people possess

To know if we really are not attached to this dunyā, we can test ourselves and see whether we become upset and flustered when we lose something worldly, or if we become extremely happy when we gain something worldly. Remember, this is not limited to money and objects; it also applies to popularity and reputation regarding worldly things.

[1] Nahjul Balāghah, Sermon 82

Heaven and Hell

Heaven and Hell are the last stops in the journey of our life. Heaven is the reward for those who believed in the truth and did good actions. On the other hand, Hell is the punishment for those who denied, altered or corrupted the truth, and did evil actions that resulted in mischief and disorder, and never repented.

In this lesson we will learn about the features of Heaven and Hell, and see how best we can achieve Heaven and avoid Hell.

Heaven and Hell reflect the realities of our own actions

From an Islamic point of view, each action has a worldly appearance as well as a reality that most of us in this world cannot see. The worldly appearance is what is seen in this world and may or may not be the same as the reality of the action. For example, in the Qur'ān, Allah (swt), the Exalted, says about taking the rights and possessions of orphans:

> "Behold, those who sinfully devour the possessions of orphans but fill their bellies with fire: for [in the life to come] they will have to endure a blazing flame!" {4:10}

The same applies to good actions. In a ḥadīth from the Prophet (s), it is mentioned that every mention of a name of Allah (swt), the Exalted, is like a brick, which is used to build your house or palace in Heaven. The more one remembers and recites dhikr, the bigger the palace the angels build for that person in Heaven.
The realities of our evil actions can be canceled out through repentance and so we should not lose hope if we have sinned in the past.

The realities of our good actions may also be destroyed if we 'burn' them through sins or evil characteristics like anger or jealousy. So we should not be proud and should never assume we have done enough for our Hereafter.

Our Heaven and our Hell expand or shrink based on our actions - the more good actions we perform, the bigger our place and pleasures in Heaven and vice versa. The existence of both Heaven and Hell are as a result of our choices and actions. If it was not so, then there would be no purpose in being given the ability to know and choose between right and wrong.

A Description of Heaven

It is impossible to describe the real picture of Heaven. Every beautiful thing which we find in this world is lower and of lesser value compared to the bounties of Heaven. The Noble Qurʿān has described Heaven in 76 āyāt in a way that we gain a limited understanding of the blessings we may enjoy there. However, the reality of Heaven is beyond our imagination. What we know is limited by language, imagination, and the capacity of our souls to understand.

The bounties of heaven have been described in the following way for the people of heaven:

1. The greatest bliss in Heaven will be Allah's proximity.
2. They will receive numerous kinds of tasty foods and drinks (including fruits) in abundance.
3. They will have full comfort, security, and stability. There will be no pain or fear of anything-no death, disease, poverty, nor distress.
4. They will live in big castles. These castles will have beautiful, big gardens, streams, rivers, and many other things which we cannot imagine.
5. They will enjoy many kinds of entertainment.
6. They will get anything they would like to have. Of course, given that they are in heaven, they would never want anything contrary to Allah's will. That is why once Allah decrees that someone must be in hell, the people of paradise will never request Allah for that person to be in heaven.
7. They will be allowed to visit the Noble Prophet (s) and Imāms (ʿa) and any other person they would like to meet.
8. They can invite the Noble Prophet (s), Imāms (ʿa) and many other guests all together at one time.

The Noble Qurʿān and the narrations summarize the blessings of Heaven in the following words:

"No person knows what enjoyment of the eyes are kept hidden in Heaven for them as a reward for their good deeds." {32:17}

"I have kept ready for my servants what no eye has ever looked at and no ear has ever heard, nor has any heart ever imagined." [1] -Ḥadīth al-Qudsī (narrated from Allah (swt) to the Prophet (s))

The beautiful and precious things of this world Allah provides us with are just small samples to give us some idea of Heaven.

A Description of Hell

Hell is a deep, wide, and large pit. In it there will be various kinds of punishments, pains, troubles, hardships, and calamities. They will be such that we cannot even imagine them.It is the opposite extreme to Heaven. There will be no room for peace, happiness, and comfort. Here are some of the tortures (punishments) the offenders face in Hell, as mentioned in the Noble Qurʿān:

The food of the people of Hell will be a bitter and thorny fruit called Zaqquūm, which will be melted in fire like copper. Zaqqūm will boil in the stomachs of proud disbelievers like water boiling or like olive oil heated over fierce fire. Then this boiling water will be poured on their heads which will melt all the outer and inner organs of the sinners. Allah (swt) says in the Qurʾān:

"Indeed those who defy our signs, we shall soon make them enter a fire; as often as their skin become scorched, we shall replace them with other skin, so that they may taste the punishment. Indeed Allah is All-Mighty, All-Wise" {4:56}.

[1] Biḥār al-Anwār, Vol. 8, P. 92

The Duration of Stay in Heaven Or Hell

It is mentioned in some of our most famous books of narrations that a companion called Abū Hāshim asked Imām Ṣādiq (ʿa) why the dwelling in Heaven or Hell will be permanent? The Imām (ʿa) replied:

"The people of Hell will live in Hell forever because their intention in the world was that if they could live in the world forever, they would disobey God forever. Likewise, the reason why the people of Heaven will live there permanently is that their intention in the world was that if they could live in the world forever, they would always obey God and would never defy his commandments." [1]

Therefore, one's intention can result in the permanent residence of the people of Heaven in Heaven and the permanent dwelling of the people of Hell in Hell. Allah (swt) knows our intentions the best.

Some people are hardened criminals and deliberate deniers of truth. Despite Allah (swt) providing them with numerous opportunities to reform and receive His special mercy, they refused to take them. Even if they were brought back into the world after seeing the Fire, they would still return to their old ways. They are examples who will remain in Hell forever and are described in the following āyah:

> "Those who engaged in disbelief and called Our signs lies are the people of Hellfire; they shall dwell in it eternally." {2:39}

However, some punishments are short in duration or less painful while others last longer and more severe. The wrongdoers' sins are not the same either in quantity or quality, and the punishment awarded them also cannot be the same.They will either spend an appropriate amount of time in Hellfire or receive the kindness and forgiveness of God. Therefore, some people will leave Hell after a certain time which only Allah (swt), the Exalted knows.

[1] Biḥār al-Anwār, Vol. 67, P. 210

However, as for Heaven, whoever enters it will remain there forever. This is a sign of the Mercy of Allah (swt), the Exalted. One can only enter Heaven if they are in a state of complete purity. Once they have achieved this state, they deserve to stay in Heaven eternally.

"Who will inherit Heaven: they will dwell therein (forever)." {23:11}

FINAL WORD

We ask Allah, our Creator and Nurturer, the One on whom we are absolutely and completely dependent, to guide us to the Truth and enable us to reach our true purpose, and grant us an eternal above in His Paradise.

The End

www.ingramcontent.com/pod-product-compliance
Lightning Source LLC
Chambersburg PA
CBHW030301100526
44590CB00012B/468
9781922583628